Yes to a Global Ethic

Yes to a Global Ethic

Edited by Hans Küng

CONTINUUM · NEW YORK

1996

The Continuum Publishing Company
370 Lexington Avenue
New York, NY 10017

Contributions not originally written in English have been
translated by John Bowden.

First published in German as *Ja zum Weltethos.
Perspektiven für die Suche nach Orientierung*, by
R. Piper GmbH & Co KG Munich 1995.

© R. Piper GmbH & Co KG Munich 1995

Translations © John Bowden 1996

Library of Congress Cataloging-in-Publication Data

Ja zum Weltethos. English.
   Yes to a global ethic/edited by Hans Küng.
     p. cm.
   ISBN 0–8264–0907–5 (pbk.)
    1. Ethics. 2. Religion and ethics. 3. Parliament of
the World's Religions (1993 ; Chicago. Ill.).
Declaration on a global ethic.
   I. Küng, Hans, 1928– . II. Title.
BJ1125.J3813 1996
170'.44—dc20   95–482 55
                                   CIP

Printed in Great Britain

Contents

Contents

Contents

To encourage all those who
throughout the world, despite disappointments,
steadfastly work for greater humanity
in things great and small

Will a Global Ethic Prevail?

HANS KÜNG

Is it an illusion to think that a change of attitude towards a global ethic could be achieved at a world level? In our world, does it look as if such a change could ever come about? At least two things would seem certain. Hardly anyone disputes that we still live in an age which is torn apart by religion and politics, which is full of war and conflict and at the same time lacking in orientation, an age in which many moral authorities have lost credibility, institutions have been caught up in the maelstrom of far-reaching crises of identity, and many criteria and norms have slipped. And hardly anyone disputes the need for a new social consensus: reflection on a minimum of humane values, basic attitudes and criteria. How are parents and teachers to bring up children if they do not know what they are to go by themselves? How are schools to cope with the readiness to use violence, which has increased so strongly? How is our society to become more human again? People say that this is necessary, but many of them doubt that it can happen in practice.

Many people also doubt, because often it is the religions which violate the commandments and norms that they themselves propagate. All over the world, religious convictions are often the cause, not of peace, understanding and reconciliation, but of war, intolerance and fanaticism. There are fundamentalist tendencies in all religions, but at present they are making themselves felt in a particularly cruel way in Muslim countries. This causes anxiety and forces others to draw dividing lines. But before we point at fundamentalism in other religions, it is better to fight its causes where we are.

Despite all this, men and women with a religious commitment all over the world have not lost hope: wherever they can be activated – whether in Poland or in South Africa, in the Philippines or in South America – the religions are still a spiritual force which could change the face of the earth for the better. A clear sign of this was the gathering of many thousands of men and women of peace in Chicago in 1993, when for the second time in the history of the religions a Parliament of the World's Religions was convened. On 4 September 1993 this Parliament passed a 'Declaration toward a Global Ethic', in which people of very different religious backgrounds for the first time agreed on a minimum of irrevocable directives which they were already affirming in their own traditions.

From the beginning, it was clear that a global ethic does not mean a new global ideology, or even an attempt to arrive at one uniform religion. The call for a global ethic does not aim to replace the supreme ethical demands of each individual religion with an ethical minimalism; it is not meant to take the place of the Torah, the Sermon on the Mount, the Qur'an, the Bhagavadgita, the Discourses of the Buddha or the Sayings of Confucius. Nor does the 'Declaration toward a Global Ethic' aim to invent a new morality and then impose it on the various religions from outside (and even from the 'West'). It simply aims to make known what religions in West and East, North and South already hold in common, but is so often obscured by numerous 'dogmatic' disputes and intolerable self-opinionatedness. In short, the 'Declaration toward a Global Ethic' seeks to emphasize the minimal ethic which is absolutely necessary for human survival. It is not directed against anyone, but invites all, believers and also non-believers, to adopt this ethic and live in accordance with it.

This 'Declaration' is a counterpoint of hope. It is a counterpoint against the fatalistic view that nothing can be done in matters of ethics, far less in matters of religion. In the 'Declaration', men and women from every possible religious and ethical tradition on this globe have expressed their readiness to change conditions on this earth out of religious conviction. In so doing they have established a sign of hope that a global change of consciousness is possible.

But how is such a global ethic to prevail? As in the question of human rights or ecology, peace and disarmament, and the partnership of men and women, this will happen in a very complex and long-drawn-out process of a change in consciousness. Pioneer thinkers have a part to play in it, as do the first activists and group initiatives: the scholars who think through the problems and the media which ensure mass communication, but also the parties, associations and churches who could gain more credibility if they made this concern their own. Nor of course are we to forget schools and places of education which are responsible for the continuous work of training ever new generations, and finally also politicians and parliaments who could formulate a charter of basic human obligations along the same lines as a charter of basic human rights – a concern which was already expressed in the debate on human rights in the parliament of the French Revolution in 1789. All the cynics of our day should be asked: weren't many of those who decades ago called for steps towards disarmament, ecological concern in the business world, and thinking in partnership between men and women also mocked for their supposed illusions? And hasn't a change of consciousness become a reality in all these three areas, already bringing about many real changes, though of course these are still far from adequate? All this is already in line with a global ethic.

The present book presupposes that there are sufficient people on this globe who believe in a change in the ethical sphere, and here in particular still believe that religions have the power to change the hearts of many for good. As representatives of countless others, here the voices of international figures from the world of politics, culture and religion are to be heard. In inviting them, the editor had no intention of aiming at some mechanically proportional representation. All those who contributed were invited primarily to speak for themselves, and were approached because they already had a manifest commitment to a global ethic. They all see the problems from their quite specific perspectives, which is what they were explicitly invited to do. The aim was neither a 'balance' of religions or cultural orientations, or uniformity of presentation. The contributors were to reflect the problems from their quite particular situation; from their continental, cultural and religious perspective. The forms were deliberately intended to be different: a short letter, a brief statement, a direct commentary on the 'Declaration' or a lengthy essay to support the cause. And indeed it is good that the forms and the reactions in this book have proved so pleasantly different.

Taken together, all these very different voices witness impressively to the fact that in the matter of a global ethic a growing awareness is already developing in many religions and cultures. The common factor in all contributions is that for the sake of peace among humankind at both a local level (in countless 'multi-cultural' and 'multi-religious' cities) and a global level (in global communication, the global economy, global ecology and global politics), reflection on an ethic common to all human beings is more than ever necessary.

At this point I would like to offer my deepest thanks to all the contributors for what they have said about a global ethic. It was clear to me that all those whom I approached had far too many demands on them. For that very reason it was by no means a matter of course that they would be willing to be involved in this project at all. However, I was glad to see that most of those whom I approached accepted my invitation spontaneously because they wanted to offer their own quite personal support to the cause of a global ethic for the sake of the future of the world community. Moreover I hope that the positions represented here will encourage countless men and women locally, in family, community and school, and in education at all levels, to devote themselves to those ethical standards which unite men and women of all religions and cultures.

To end with, a look towards the future. After my own

Global Responsibility (1991), and *A Global Ethic* (1993), which I edited with my Tübingen colleague Karl-Josef Kuschel, here is a third volume in English on the topic of a global ethic. In the foreseeable future Karl-Josef Kuschel will edit another volume, *Scholars Reflect on a Global Ethic*, in which representatives of the religions, business ethics, education, philosophy, anthropology, law and sociology will be invited to express their views from the perspective of their disciplines.

Alongside this, I myself want to continue the basic theological work. After *Judaism* (1992) and *Christianity* (1995), if I am allowed to do so, I want first to finish the project of 'The Religious Situation of Our Time' with the volume on *Islam*. All this in the firm hope that as a result of the commitment of an increasing number of people throughout the world, a global ethic will finally prevail.

Tübingen, June 1995

THE PARLIAMENT OF THE WORLD'S RELIGIONS

Declaration toward a Global Ethic

*The text entitled 'Introduction' was produced by an Editorial Committee of the 'Council' of the Parliament of the World's Religions in Chicago on the basis of the Declaration composed in Tübingen (here headed 'Principles'). It was meant to serve as a brief summary of the Declaration for publicity purposes. At the same time it was intended to be read aloud in public. So this text was read out publicly at the solemn concluding plenary on 4 September 1993 in Grant Park, Chicago: a number of passages were greeted with spontaneous applause by the audience of thousands.

Introduction*

The world is in agony. The agony is so pervasive and urgent that we are compelled to name its manifestations so that the depth of this pain may be made clear.

Peace eludes us . . . the planet is being destroyed . . . neighbours live in fear . . . women and men are estranged from each other . . . children die!

This is abhorrent!

We condemn the abuses of Earth's ecosystems.

We condemn the poverty that stifles life's potential; the hunger that weakens the human body; the economic disparities that threaten so many families with ruin.

We condemn the social disarray of the nations; the disregard for justice which pushes citizens to the margin; the anarchy overtaking our communities; and the insane death of children from violence. In particular we condemn aggression and hatred in the name of religion.

But this agony need not be.

It need not be because the basis for an ethic already exists. This ethic offers the possibility of a better individual and global order, and leads individuals away from despair and societies away from chaos.

We are women and men who have embraced the precepts and practices of the world's religions.

We affirm that a common set of core values is found in the teachings of the religions, and that these form the basis of a global ethic.

We affirm that this truth is already known, but yet to be lived in heart and action.

We affirm that there is an irrevocable, unconditional norm for all areas of life, for families and communities, for races, nations and religions. There already exist ancient guidelines for human behaviour which are found in the teachings of the religions of the world and which are the conditions for a sustainable world order.

We declare:

We are interdependent. Each of us depends on the well-being of the whole, and so we have respect for the community of living beings, for people, animals, and plants, and for the preservation of Earth, the air, water and soil.

We take individual responsibility for all we do. All our decisions, actions, and failures to act have consequences.

We must treat others as we wish others to treat us. We make a commitment to respect life and dignity, individuality and diversity, so that every person is treated humanely, without exception. We must have patience and acceptance. We must be able to forgive, learning from the past but never allowing ourselves to be enslaved by memories of hate. Opening our *hearts to one another, we must sink our narrow differences for the cause of world community, practising a culture of solidarity and relatedness.*

We consider humankind our family. We must strive to be kind and generous. We must not live for ourselves alone, but should also serve others, never forgetting the children, the aged, the poor, the suffering, the disabled, the refugees, and the lonely. No person should ever be considered or treated as a second-class citizen, or be exploited in any way whatsoever. There should be equal partnership between men and women. We must not commit any kind of sexual immorality. We must put behind us all forms of domination or abuse.

We commit ourselves to a culture of non-violence, respect, justice and peace. We shall not oppress, injure, torture, or kill other human beings, forsaking violence as a means of settling differences.

We must strive for a just social and economic order, in which everyone has an equal chance to reach full potential as a human being. We must speak and act truthfully and with compassion, dealing fairly with all, and avoiding prejudice and hatred. We must not steal. We must move beyond the dominance of greed for power, prestige, money and consumption to make a just and peaceful world. Earth cannot be changed for the better unless the consciousness of individuals is changed first. We pledge to increase our awareness by disciplining our minds, by meditation, by prayer, or by positive thinking. Without risk and a readiness to sacrifice there can be no fundamental change in our situation. Therefore we commit ourselves to this global ethic, to understanding one another, and to socially-beneficial, peace-fostering, and nature-friendly ways of life.

We invite all people, whether religious or not, to do the same.

The Principles of a Global Ethic

Our world is experiencing a *fundamental crisis*, a crisis in global economy, global ecology, and global politics. The lack of a grand vision, the tangle of unresolved problems, political paralysis, mediocre political leadership with little insight or foresight, and in general too little sense for the commonweal are seen everywhere. Too many old answers to new challenges.

Hundreds of millions of human beings on our planet increasingly suffer from unemployment, poverty, hunger, and the destruction of their families. Hope for a lasting peace among nations slips away from us. There are tensions between the sexes and generations. Children die, kill, and are killed. More and more countries are shaken by corruption in politics and business. It is increasingly difficult to live together peacefully in our cities because of social, racial, and ethnic conflicts, the abuse of drugs, organized crime, and even anarchy. Even neighbours often live in fear of one another. Our planet continues to be ruthlessly plundered. A collapse of the ecosystem threatens us.

Time and again we see leaders and members of *religions* incite aggression, fanaticism, hate, and xenophobia – even inspire and legitimate violent and bloody conflicts. Religion often is misused for purely power-political goals, including war. We are filled with disgust.

We condemn these blights and declare that they need not be. An *ethic* already exists within the religious teachings of the world which can counter the global distress. Of course this ethic provides no direct solution for all the immense problems of the world, but it does supply the moral foundation for a better individual and global order: a *vision* which can lead women and men away from despair, and society away from chaos.

We are persons who have committed ourselves to the precepts and practices of the world's religions. We confirm that there is already a consensus among the religions which can be the basis for a global ethic – a minimal *fundamental consensus* concerning binding *values*, irrevocable *standards*, and fundamental *moral attitudes*.

I. No new global order without a new global ethic

We women and men of various religions and regions of Earth therefore address all people, religious and non-religious. We wish to express the following convictions which we hold in common.

- We *all* have a *responsibility for a better global order*.
- Our involvement for the sake of human rights, freedom, justice, peace, and the preservation of Earth is absolutely necessary.
- Our different religious and cultural traditions must not prevent our common involvement in opposing all forms of inhumanity and working for greater humaneness.
- The principles expressed in this global ethic can be affirmed by all persons with ethical convictions, whether religiously grounded or not.

As *religious and spiritual persons* we base our lives on an Ultimate Reality, and draw spiritual power and hope therefrom, in trust, in prayer or meditation, in word or silence. We have a special responsibility for the welfare of all humanity and care for the planet Earth. We do not consider ourselves better than other women and men, but we trust that the ancient wisdom of our religions can point the way for the future.

After two world wars and the end of the cold war, the collapse of fascism and nazism, the shaking to the foundations of communism and colonialism, humanity has entered a new phase of its history. Today we possess sufficient economic, cultural, and spiritual resources to introduce a better global order, but old and new *ethnic, national, social, economic, and religious tensions* threaten the peaceful building of a better world. We have experienced greater technological progress than ever before, yet we see that world-wide poverty, hunger, death of children, unemployment, misery, and the destruction of nature have not diminished but rather have increased. Many peoples are threatened with economic ruin, social disarray, political marginalization, ecological catastrophe, and moral collapse.

In such a dramatic global situation humanity needs a *vision of peoples living peacefully together*, of ethnic and ethical groupings and of religions sharing responsibility for the care of Earth. A vision rests on hopes, goals, ideals, standards. But all over the world these have slipped from our hands. Yet we are convinced that, despite their frequent abuses and failures, it is the communities of faith who bear a responsibility to demonstrate that such hopes, ideals, and standards can be guarded, grounded and lived. This is especially true in the modern state. Guarantees of freedom of conscience and religion are necessary, but they do not substitute for binding values, convictions, and norms which are valid for all humans regardless of their social origin, sex, skin colour, language, or religion.

We are convinced of the fundamental unity of the human family on Earth. We recall the 1948 Universal Declaration of Human Rights of the United Nations. What it formally proclaimed on the level of *rights* we wish to confirm and deepen here from the perspective of an *ethic*: the full realization of the intrinsic dignity of the human person, the inalienable freedom and equality in principle of all humans, and the necessary solidarity and interdependence of all humans with each other.

On the basis of personal experiences and the burdensome history of our planet we have learned

- that a better global order cannot be created or enforced by laws, prescriptions, and conventions alone;
- that the realization of peace, justice, and the protection of

earth depends on the insight and readiness of men and women to act justly;

- that action in favour of rights and freedoms presumes a consciousness of responsibility and duty, and that therefore both the minds and hearts of women and men must be addressed;
- that rights without morality cannot long endure, and that there will be *no better global order without a global ethic.*

By a global ethic we do not mean a global ideology or a *single unified religion* beyond all existing religions, and certainly not the domination of one religion over all others. By a global ethic we mean a *fundamental consensus on binding values, irrevocable standards, and personal attitudes.* Without such a fundamental consensus on an ethic, sooner or later every community will be threatened by chaos or dictatorship, and individuals will despair.

II. A fundamental demand: Every human being must be treated humanely

We are all fallible, imperfect men and women with limitations and defects. We know the reality of evil. Precisely because of this, we feel compelled for the sake of global welfare to express what the fundamental elements of a global ethic should be – for individuals as well as for communities and organizations, for states as well as for the religions themselves. We trust that our often millennia-old religious and ethical traditions provide an ethic which is convincing and practical for *all women and men of good will*, religious and non-religious.

At the same time we know that our various religious and ethical traditions often offer very different bases of what is helpful and what is unhelpful for men and women, what is right and what is wrong, what is good and what is evil. We do not wish to gloss over or ignore the serious differences among the individual religions. However, they should not hinder us from proclaiming publicly *those things which we already hold* in common and which we jointly affirm, each on the basis of our own religious or ethical grounds.

We know that religions cannot solve the environmental, economic, political, and social problems of Earth. However, they can provide what obviously cannot be attained by economic plans, political programmes or legal regulations alone: *a change in* the inner orientation, the whole mentality, *the hearts of people*, and a conversion from a false path to a new orientation for life. Humankind urgently needs social and ecological reforms, but it needs *spiritual renewal* just as urgently. As religious or spiritual persons we commit ourselves to this task. The spiritual powers of the religions can offer a fundamental sense of trust, a ground of meaning, ultimate standards, and a spiritual home. Of course religions are credible only when they eliminate those conflicts which spring from the religions themselves, dismantling mutual arrogance, mistrust, prejudice, and even hostile images, and thus demonstrate respect for the traditions, holy places, feasts, and rituals of people who believe differently.

Now as before, *women and men are treated inhumanely* all over the world. They are robbed of their opportunities and their freedom; their human rights are trampled underfoot; their dignity is disregarded. But might does not make right! In the face of all humanity our religious and ethical convictions demand that *every human being must be treated humanely*!

This means that every human being without distinction of age, sex, race, skin colour, physical or mental ability, language, religion, political view, or national or social origin possesses an inalienable and *untouchable dignity*. And everyone, the individual as well as the state, is therefore obliged to honour this dignity and protect it. Humans must always be the subjects of rights, must be ends, never mere means, never objects of commercialization and industrialization in economics, politics and media, in research institutes, and industrial corporations. No one stands 'above good and evil' — no human being, no social class, no influential interest group, no cartel, no police apparatus, no army, and no state. On the contrary; possessed of reason and conscience, every human is obliged to behave in a genuinely human fashion, to *do good and avoid evil*!

It is the intention of this Global Ethic to clarify what this means. In it we wish to recall irrevocable, unconditional ethical norms. These should not be bonds and chains, but helps and supports for people to find and realize once again their lives' directions, orientations, and meaning.

There is a principle which is found and has persisted in many religious and ethical traditions of humankind for thousands of years: *What you do not wish done to yourself, do not do to others!* Or in positive terms: *What you wish done to yourself, do to others!* This should be the irrevocable, unconditional norm for all areas of life, for families and communities, for races, nations and religions.

Every form of egoism should be rejected: all selfishness, whether individual or collective, whether in the form of class thinking, racism, nationalism, or sexism. We condemn these because they prevent humans from being authentically human. Self-determination and self-realization are thoroughly legitimate so long as they are not separated from human self-responsibility and global responsibility, that is, from responsibility for fellow humans and for the planet Earth.

This principle implies very concrete standards to which we humans should hold firm. From it arise *four broad, ancient guidelines* for human behaviour which are found in most of the religions of the world.

III. Four irrevocable directives

1. *Commitment to a culture of non-violence and respect for life*

Numberless women and men of all regions and religions strive to lead lives not determined by egoism but by commitment to their fellow humans and to the world around them. Nevertheless, all over the world we find endless hatred, envy, jealousy and violence, not only between individuals but also between social and ethnic groups, between classes, races, nations, and religions. The use of violence, drug trafficking and organized crime, often equipped with new technical possibilities, has reached global proportions. Many places are still ruled by terror 'from above'; dictators oppress their own people, and institutional violence is widespread. Even in some countries where laws exist to protect individual freedoms, prisoners are tortured, men and women are mutilated, hostages are killed.

(a) In the great ancient religious and ethical traditions of humankind we find the directive: *You shall not kill*! Or in positive terms: *Have respect for life*! Let us reflect anew on the consequences of this ancient directive: all people have a right to life, safety, and the free development of personality in so far as they do not injure the rights of others. No one has the right physically or psychically to torture, injure, much less kill, any other human being. And no people, no state, no race, no religion has the right to hate, to discriminate against, to 'cleanse', to exile, much less to liquidate a 'foreign' minority which is different in behaviour or holds different beliefs.

(b) Of course, wherever there are humans there will be conflicts. Such conflicts, however, should be resolved without violence within a framework of justice. This is true for states as well as for individuals. Persons who hold political power must work within the framework of a just order and commit themselves to the most non-violent, peaceful solutions possible. And they should work for this within an international order of peace which itself has need of protection and defence against perpetrators of violence. Armament is a mistaken path; disarmament is the commandment of the times. Let no one be deceived: There is no survival for humanity without global peace!

(c) Young people must learn at home and in school that violence may not be a means of settling differences with others. Only thus can a *culture of non-violence* be created.

(d) A human person is infinitely precious and must be unconditionally protected. But likewise the *lives of animals and plants* which inhabit this planet with us deserve protection, preservation, and care. Limitless exploitation of the natural foundations of life, ruthless destruction of the biosphere, and militarization of the cosmos are all outrages. As human beings we have a special responsibility – especially with a view to future generations – for Earth and the cosmos, for the air, water, and soil. We are *all intertwined together* in this cosmos and we are all dependent on each other. Each one of us depends on the welfare of all. Therefore the dominance of humanity over nature and the cosmos must not be encouraged. Instead we must cultivate living in harmony with nature and the cosmos.

(e) To be authentically human in the spirit of our great religious and ethical traditions means that in public as well as in private life we must be concerned for others and ready to help. We must never be ruthless and brutal. Every people, every race, every religion must show tolerance and respect – indeed high appreciation – for every other. Minorities need protection and support, whether they be racial, ethnic, or religious.

2. Commitment to a culture of solidarity and a just economic order

Numberless men and women of all regions and religions strive to live their lives in solidarity with one another and to work for authentic fulfilment of their vocations. Nevertheless, all over the world we find endless hunger, deficiency, and need. Not only individuals, but especially unjust institutions and structures are responsible for these tragedies. Millions of people are without work; millions are exploited by poor wages, forced to the edges of society, with their possibilities for the future destroyed. In many lands the gap between the poor and the rich, between the powerful and the powerless is immense. We live in a world in which totalitarian state socialism as well as unbridled capitalism have hollowed out and destroyed many ethical and spiritual values. A materialistic mentality breeds greed for unlimited profit and a grasping for endless plunder. These demands claim more and more of the community's resources without obliging the individual to contribute more. The cancerous social evil of corruption thrives in the developing countries and in the developed countries alike.

(a) In the great ancient religious and ethical traditions of humankind we find the directive: *You shall not steal*! Or in positive terms: *Deal honestly and fairly*! Let us reflect anew on the consequences of this ancient directive: No one has the right to rob or dispossess in any way whatsoever any other person or the commonweal. Further, no one has the right to use her or his possessions without concern for the needs of society and Earth.

(b) Where extreme poverty reigns, helplessness and despair spread, and theft occurs again and again for the sake of survival. Where power and wealth are accumulated ruthlessly, feelings of envy, resentment, and deadly hatred and rebellion inevitably well up in the disadvantaged and marginalized. This leads to a vicious circle of violence and counter-violence. Let no one be deceived: There is no global peace without global justice!

(c) Young people must learn at home and in school that property, limited though it may be, carries with it an obligation, and that its uses should at the same time serve the common good. Only thus can a *just economic order* be built up.

(d) If the plight of the poorest billions of humans on this planet, particularly women and children, is to be improved, the world economy must be structured more justly. Individual good deeds, and assistance projects, indispensable though they be, are insufficient. The participation of all states and the authority of international organizations are needed to build just economic institutions.

A solution which can be supported by all sides must be

sought for the debt crisis and the poverty of the dissolving Second World, and even more the Third World. Of course conflicts of interest are unavoidable. In the developed countries, a distinction must be made between necessary and limitless consumption, between socially beneficial and non-beneficial uses of property, between justified and unjustified uses of natural resources, and between a profit-only and a socially beneficial and ecologically oriented market economy. Even the developing nations must search their national consciences.

Wherever those ruling threaten to repress those ruled, wherever institutions threaten persons, and wherever might oppresses right, we have an obligation to resist – whenever possible non-violently.

(e) To be authentically human in the spirit of our great religious and ethical traditions means the following:

We must utilize economic and political power for *service to humanity* instead of misusing it in ruthless battles for domination. We must develop a spirit of compassion with those who suffer, with special care for the children, the aged, the poor, the disabled, the refugees, and the lonely.

We must cultivate *mutual respect* and consideration, so as to reach a reasonable balance of interests, instead of thinking only of unlimited power and unavoidable competitive struggles.

We must value *a sense of moderation and modesty* instead of an unquenchable greed for money, prestige, and consumption! In greed humans lose their 'souls', their freedom, their composure, their inner peace, and thus that which makes them human.

3. Commitment to a culture of tolerance and a life of truthfulness

Numberless women and men of all regions and religions strive to lead lives of honesty and truthfulness. Nevertheless, all over the world we find endless lies and deceit, swindling and hypocrisy, ideology and demagoguery:

- Politicians and business people who use lies as a means to success;
- Mass media which spread ideological propaganda instead of accurate reporting, misinformation instead of information, cynical commercial interest instead of loyalty to the truth;
- Scientists and researchers who give themselves over to morally questionable ideological or political programmes or to economic interest groups, or who justify research which violates fundamental ethical values;
- Representatives of religions who dismiss other religions as of little value and who preach fanaticism and intolerance instead of respect and understanding.

(a) In the great ancient religious and ethical traditions of humankind we find the directive: *You shall not lie*! Or in positive terms: *Speak and act truthfully*! Let us reflect anew on the consequences of this ancient directive: No woman or man, no institution, no state or church or religious community has the right to speak lies to other humans.

(b) This is especially true:

- For those who work in the *mass media*, to whom we entrust the freedom to report for the sake of truth and to whom we thus grant the office of guardian. They do not stand above morality but have the obligation to respect human dignity, human rights, and fundamental values. They are duty-bound to objectivity, fairness, and the preservation of human dignity. They have no right to intrude into individuals' private spheres, to manipulate public opinion, or to distort reality.
- For *artists, writers, and scientists*, to whom we entrust artistic and academic freedom. They are not exempt from general ethical standards and must serve the truth;
- For the *leaders of countries, politicians, and political parties* to whom we entrust our own freedoms. When they lie in the faces of their people, when they manipulate the truth, or when they are guilty of venality or ruthlessness in domestic or foreign affairs, they forsake their credibility and deserve

to lose their offices and their voters. Conversely, public opinion should support those politicians who dare to speak the truth to the people at all times.

- Finally, for *representatives of religion*. When they stir up prejudice, hatred, and enmity towards those of different belief, or even incite or legitimate religious wars, they deserve the condemnation of humankind and the loss of their adherents.

Let no one be deceived. There is no global justice without truthfulness and humaneness!

(c) Young people must learn at home and in school to think, speak, and act *truthfully*. They have a right to information and education to be able to make the decisions that will form their lives. Without an ethical formation they will hardly be able to distinguish the important from the unimportant. In the daily flood of information, ethical standards will help them discern when opinions are portrayed as facts, interests veiled, tendencies exaggerated, and facts twisted.

(d) To be authentically human in the spirit of our great religious and ethical traditions means the following:

- We must not confuse freedom with arbitrariness or pluralism with indifference to *truth*.
- We must cultivate *truthfulness* in all our relationships instead of dishonesty, dissembling, and opportunism.
- We must *constantly seek truth* and incorruptible sincerity instead of spreading ideological or partisan half-truths.
- We must courageously *serve the truth* and we must remain *constant and trustworthy*, instead of yielding to opportunistic accommodation to life.

4. Commitment to a culture of equal rights and partnership between men and women

Numberless men and women of all regions and religions strive to live their lives in a spirit of partnership and responsible action in the areas of love, sexuality, and family. Nevertheless all over the world there are condemnable forms of patriarchy, domination of one sex over the other, exploitation of women, sexual misuse of children, and forced prostitution. Too frequently, social inequities force women and even children into prostitution as a means of survival – particularly in less developed countries.

(a) In the great ancient religious and ethical traditions of humankind we find the directive: *You shall not commit sexual immorality*! Or in positive terms: *Respect and love one another*! Let us reflect anew on the consequences of this ancient directive: No one has the right to degrade others to mere sex objects, to lead them into or hold them in sexual dependency.

(b) We condemn sexual exploitation and sexual discrimination as one of the worst forms of human degradation. We have the duty to resist wherever the domination of one sex over the other is preached – even in the name of religious conviction; wherever sexual exploitation is tolerated, wherever prostitution is fostered or children are misused. Let no one be deceived: There is no authentic humaneness without a living together in partnership!

(c) Young people must learn at home and in school that sexuality is not a negative, destructive, or exploitative force, but creative and affirmative. Sexuality as a life-affirming shaper of community can only be effective when partners accept the responsibilities of caring for one another's happiness.

(d) The relationship between women and men should be characterized not by patronizing behaviour or exploitation, but by love, partnership, and trustworthiness. Human fulfilment is not identical with sexual pleasure. Sexuality should express and reinforce a loving relationship lived by equal partners.

Some religious traditions know the ideal of a voluntary renunciation of the full use of sexuality. Voluntary renunciation also can be an expression of identity and meaningful fulfilment.

(e) The social institution of marriage, despite all its cultural and religious variety, is characterized by love, loyalty, and permanence. It aims at and should guarantee security and mutual support to husband, wife, and child. It should secure the rights of all family members. All lands and cultures should develop economic and social relationships which will enable marriage and family life worthy of human beings, especially for older people. Children have a right of access to education. Parents should not exploit children, nor children parents. Their relationships should reflect mutual respect, appreciation, and concern.

(f) To be authentically human in the spirit of our great religious and ethical traditions means the following:

We need mutual respect, *partnership*, and understanding, instead of patriarchal domination and degradation, which are expressions of violence and engender counter-violence.

We need mutual concern, tolerance, readiness for reconciliation, and *love*, instead of any form of possessive lust or sexual misuse.

Only what has already been experienced in personal and familial relationships can be practised on the level of nations and religions.

IV. A transformation of consciousness

Historical experience demonstrates the following: Earth cannot be changed for the better unless we achieve a transformation in the consciousness of individuals and in public life. The possibilities for transformation have already been glimpsed in areas such as war and peace, economy, and ecology, where in recent decades fundamental changes have taken place. This transformation must also be achieved in the area of ethics and values! Every individual has intrinsic dignity and inalienable rights, and each also has an inescapable responsibility for what she or he does and does not do. All our decisions and deeds, even our omissions and failures, have consequences.

Keeping this sense of responsibility alive, deepening it and passing it on to future generations, is the special task of religions. We are realistic about what we have achieved in this consensus, and so we urge that the following be observed.

1. A universal consensus on *many disputed ethical questions* (from bio- and sexual ethics through mass media and scientific ethics to economic and political ethics) will be difficult to attain. Nevertheless, even for many controversial questions, suitable solutions should be attainable in the spirit of the fundamental principles we have jointly developed here.

2. In many areas of life a new consciousness of ethical responsibility has already arisen. Therefore we would be pleased if as many *professions* as possible, such as those of physicians, scientists, business people, journalists, and politicians would develop up-to-date *codes of ethics* which would provide specific guidelines for the vexing questions of these particular professions.

3. Above all, we urge the various *communities of faith* to formulate their very *specific ethic*: what does each faith tradition have to say, for example, about the meaning of life and death, the enduring of suffering and the forgiveness of guilt, about selfless sacrifice and the necessity of renunciation, about compassion and joy? These will deepen, and make more specific, the already discernible global ethic.

In conclusion, we appeal to all the inhabitants of this planet. Earth cannot be changed for the better unless the consciousness of individuals is changed. We pledge to work for such transformation in individual and collective consciousness, for the awakening of our spiritual powers through reflection, meditation, prayer, or positive thinking, for a *conversion of the heart*. Together we can move mountains! Without a willingness to take risks and a readiness to sacrifice there can be no fundamental change in our situation! Therefore we commit ourselves to a common global ethic, to better mutual understanding, as well as to socially-beneficial, peace-fostering, and Earth-friendly ways of life.

We invite all men and women, whether religious or not, to do the same.

From the World of Politics and Culture

Towards a Shared Global Ethic

RICHARD VON WEIZSÄCKER

*From 1984 to 1994 the author was President of the
Federal Republic of Germany*

Fifty years ago, the United Nations was founded. The initiative
legitimately came from the victors in the Second World War.
Their main concern was to prevent a new world war in the
future. They created the Security Council as its central organ,
with the beginnings of an executive authority. Their primary
aim was to achieve the capacity to avert military threats. At the
same time the great powers protected themselves from one
another. With their monopoly of the right to veto any decision
of this most important organ of the international community,
they preserved their dominant position.

Advances and setbacks over security

Since then half a century has passed, marked by advances and
serious setbacks in the communal life of humankind. The end
of the Cold War between East and West has brought an
improvement. The Security Council is no longer, as it used to
be, *a priori* paralysed by abuse of the right to veto, often
exercised in a selfishly nationalistic way. But no conclusions
have yet been drawn from the inescapable insight that the
threat to security on earth today is by no means primarily
military. What stands in the forefront is the series of apparently insoluble emergencies caused by the headlong increase in
the world population, hunger and distress among the majority
of peoples, the wretchedness of the ever-growing stream of

refugees, the unjust exploitation of the economically weaker regions, the plundering of nature and the threat of catastrophe to the climate. No arming of superpowers can master these dangers. They are threats to security of which the founders of the United Nations had no idea fifty years ago.

In the meantime specialist organizations of UNO have been created to cope with the dangers mentioned above, like UNICEF, UNCTAD, UNDEP, UNHCR, WHO, FAO, UNESCO and so on. But they have no access to the Security Council, the centre where decisions are made. Granted, they have spoken passionately in the General Assembly and the special World Assemblies, but so far without any decisive success. Therefore the majority of the members of the international community are becoming increasingly dis-heartened and resigned.

One of the central tasks of a reform of the United Nations at the beginning of its second half-century will be not merely just to continue to counter the symptoms of the dangers to security with weapons, but to identify their causes with other than military means and to help to eradicate them, especially in the sphere of social and economic tasks, human rights and development.

Democracy lives by ethical presuppositions

Now if we are really serious about tackling the roots of these problems, we men and women, citizens of the world, cannot just look to our governments and economic centres for more wisdom and international readiness to help. At any rate in democracies with free constitutions and market economies, they tend to go by what they think to be the attitudes and wishes of us citizens. And what are these attitudes? All too often a consumer culture with a private and individualistic stamp prevails. Our personal life-style usually contributes more towards burdening than towards sparing the environ-ment. The state and governments face demands from their citizens. A sense of common responsibility for the well-being of the whole is tending to decline rather than increase. This makes a common and resolute world policy difficult for governments.

Democracy is conjured up on every side. This is necessary and right when it comes to freedom and human rights. But we must never forget that a democratic constitution lives by presuppositions which it cannot create itself. It has to protect men and women from the incursions of the state, and decisive progress has been made where this is achieved. The market is meant to satisfy our needs; it does that better than other economic systems. But neither of these has any power of integration: constitutions cannot provide basic ethical rules for society which are generally respected and desired, a readiness to do one's duty towards others in addition to having rights over against the state – and these rules are increasingly lacking.

The more strongly this lack is felt, the clearer becomes the need for guidelines and models for a just form of social life which guarantees human dignity. The quest for an ethical orientation is intensifying.

A call to the religions

Here at the same time the question of the ethical force of the religions becomes central. Many religious communities have not only been damaged by their conflicts with the irreversible modernization of life in the wake of the Enlightenment, science and technology. They have often also been damaged by their claims to truth which lead them to live in conflict with one another; the resultant tensions keep being transferred to society as a whole and thus create disturbances as well as peace.

Far more important, though, is the secularization of societies, in whose eyes religions are not to be looked to for any help because they are primarily entangled with one another in conflicts over possession of the truth.

Credibility is the issue. It can only be grounded in collaboration, in ecumenical reflection. The task of religions is not to lure the faithful in the name of their own doctrines and rules, but to make a contribution to the pacification and humanization of our society. This does not mean that dialogue and argument about the truth are to be abandoned. Their aim is to recognize how deep is the belief of the other, to take this seriously and to strengthen it. Only on this basis can a viable foundation for collaboration be created. That is the first step towards one's own ethical conduct. It provides the necessary example for society.

In our age, all developments are global: technology, science, economics, transport, politics, ecology. Only civilization is still lagging behind. Human beings have always developed the process of civilization step by step, in the framework which governed their life. From the communal dimension, through the state, the regional and the international dimension, they have had to learn to live together in a tolerable, i.e. a civilized manner. Now we face the same task at a global level. The first important steps have been taken, above all the universal human rights of the United Nations. These are directed towards the states, but the states still claim inviolability for their own inner concerns, even if they are gradually learning global rules for behaviour towards one another. Individuals must also do the same thing. The religions are called on to give effective examples from the wealth of their teachings and convictions. Jews, Christians and Muslims, Buddhists, Confucians and Hindus – all religions contain rules for common living stamped by deep experience and wisdom. Even among animists in Africa, for example, we hear the admonition: 'Even in the greatest dispute spare the life of the other.'

To make the point once again: in our ecumene there can be no question of the religions relativizing themselves in their faith in favour of a common, superficial behavioural ethic. The important thing is for them to take one another so seriously that they can give the first and most important example of peace among human beings. This peace is more than a co-existence which has merely tactical motivations; it is based on the respect of others, which is no less than the respect that one claims for oneself. Love your neighbour, for your neighbour is like you, and as self-concerned and in need of protection as you are.

Ethics is not the content of religion, but the test of its credibility. It is a task and mandate of the religions for human society. Now, as dangers and problems, interconnections and tasks are becoming global as never before in world history, there is need for a development towards a global civilization at the heart of which is a growing global ethic. Here it will be of decisive significance whether the world religions succeed in making their contribution by providing examples.

The Parliament of the World's Religions took a decisive step with the Declaration on a Global Ethic. It is necessary for all of us. Now we need to continue in this direction, adopt the content of the Declaration in open discussion, and authenticate it in word and action. Those who take their religion seriously should not stand aside.

The Destiny of Humankind is at Stake

LEV KOPELEV

The author, who was born in Kiev, is a literary critic and journalist. He was awarded the Peace Prize of the German Book Trade

Humankind lives only by being mutual
sureties for the good

Published by Marina Zvetayeva from the poem of
a nun who wanted to remain anonymous.

A global ethic! Is there such a thing? Can there be demands for humanity which are clearly understood, accepted and recognized by all human beings in all civilizations, at all levels of education?

History gives us examples

History gives us examples of this, both sorry examples and examples which give us hope. The founders of all the great religious doctrines proclaimed divine commandments and kept asserting them. The many gods of the polytheists, most of which were all too human, embodied different notions of good and evil, virtue and vice; they left it to moral thinkers to bring their moral conceptions and ideals under a common denominator. But centuries before Christ, Confucius and Lao-tse developed ethical and moral doctrines which were to be accepted universally. Sometimes these are very precise, down to the smallest detail; sometimes they have an abstract dialectical motivation, only making statements, recommending rather than enjoining. Nevertheless, in some respects they accord with the ethics of the Bible, as for example in the command 'Do not do to another what you would not want to have done to yourself.'

The Ten Commandments, the laments of the biblical prophets, Jesus' Sermon on the Mount and many parables in the Gospels and the letters of the apostles contain demands which are akin to the teachings of Buddha and Muhammad. Many of them have also been taken over by rebels who stormed heaven, modern sceptics and humane atheists.

Francis Bacon, a consistent materialist, wanted to investigate the real origins of the human world-view, its various idols. Benedict Spinoza presented his mathematical pantheistic picture of the world in the book *Ethica ordine geometrico demonstrata*. For him God and nature were an indissoluble unity, and the ethical laws were laws of nature.

The disillusioned, tragically resigned thinkers of the baroque era, who like Thomas Hobbes were convinced that men were at each other's throats like wolves, or who like George Berkeley denied the possibilities of an objective, generally valid view of the world because all that exists exists only in subjective perception and experience (*esse est percipi*), came up against the men of the Enlightenment who believed in the future. John Locke already asserted that every person is born a *tabula rasa* and that a good, well-planned education can make him reasonable and virtuous. Leibniz, Lessing and Montesquieu, Shaftesbury and Lomonossov, were convinced that one need only enlighten people and educate them rightly for the world to be reasonable and whole. In his essay 'A Postscript to Bougainville's Journey', Diderot claimed that the development of international navigation alone would bring people of different races closer together and make war simply impossible.

Kant's essay 'On Eternal Peace' was the climax of Enlightenment trust in human reason, in the imminent realization of ethical and moral principles of humanity that would embrace the world.

The development of social and political realities in subsequent centuries unleashed evil forces which were opposed to the ideals and dreams of the men of the Enlightenment. The idea of the nation which had been hopefully and fruitfully discovered by the Enlightenment and the age of Romanticism, and was asserted militantly in a new form by the French revolutionaries, was originally a unifying idea: it was to unite and hold together people of different classes or different politics by the recognition of a common language and a common historical destiny. But in the very next century, and even more in the century after, this idea degenerated into ideologies which separated and alienated, into nationalisms and chauvinisms.

The idea of the social solidarity of all workers, the dreams of freedom, equality and brotherhood, of a just social order, were often transformed into slogans in class warfare, and led enthusiastic idealists astray into reckless acts of violence. Grandiose revolutionary aims often justified the worst means of fighting, and made whole peoples fight their way from one form of violent rule to another.

The unstoppable pressure towards scientific knowledge about the biological and social nature of human beings was misused by militant nationalists and champions of an authoritarian social and political 'order', and applied in pseudo-scientific, social Darwinian and racist theories.

The colonial wars of the nineteenth century and the World War which broke out in 1914 and still has not come to an end – it has been only interrupted now and then by supposedly peaceful intervals like 1919-1939 or continued with other means, like the Cold War – seemed to have destroyed the dream of a global ethic, a peaceful understanding between peoples of different states, nations, religions and ideologies. Now events in the territories of the Soviet Union, that erstwhile world power which collapsed with such surprising rapidity, and former Yugoslavia, along with the minor wars in Asia, Africa, Central and South America, seem to be confirming the worst intimations of Friedrich Nietzsche and Oswald Spengler.

The necessary unity of science, politics and morality

But now, on the eve of a new century and millennium, against the background of global ecological dangers and world-wide criminality, hopes of a global ethic are again becoming more significant and more important than before. For now we can hope only for what Brecht called the 'gentle force of reason'.

The Parliament of the World's Religions which met in Chicago in August/September 1993, in which clergy and laity – the representatives of different religious doctrines – took part, proclaimed this need in a joint declaration of principles which begins with the words 'The world is in agony' and unequivocally states:

> We are interdependent. Each of us depends on the well-being of the whole, and so we have respect for the community of living beings, for people, animals, and plants, and for the preservation of Earth, the air, water and soil.

Such an understanding can be arrived at only through the unity of science, politics and morality.

There have been ignorant and immoral governments at all times and in all countries, and some potentates were even convinced that much knowledge only harms the power of the state. The emperor Qin Shi Huang, who had the Great Wall of China 'completed', had scholars and philosophers murdered or exiled and their writings burned. The victorious Sultan Suleiman commanded that the great library of Alexandria should be burnt to the ground, because humankind needed only one book, the Qur'an. The history of humankind is full of such power-hungry men of darkness – down to Hitler and Stalin. Weapons, banners, titles and ideologies have changed, but the principles of an immoral power have remained the same: 'All means that lead to success are good'; 'the stronger determine who is right', and suchlike.

There are also exceptions, for example the philosopher

emperors Marcus Aurelius and Frederick II of Hohenstaufen, and other kings, popes and princes who loved literature, music and the graphic arts. But better education and finer taste only made a very few rulers more just and humane.

Ignorant and immoral rulers of former times – from Troy to Hiroshima, from the campaigns of Genghis Khan to Auschwitz and Kolyma – murdered hundreds, thousands, in our century even millions of people, destroyed temples and cities, ravaged flourishing areas, exterminated whole tribes and peoples. Ignorant and immoral rulers today are in a position to annihilate billions of men and women, indeed all of humankind and all life on earth.

Nevertheless, even today there is a refusal to accept that state politics and science are absolutely different worlds, between which hardly any understanding is possible. And it is believed that humanity – i.e. justice and mercy – belongs to neither of these two worlds, that it can perhaps be the characteristic of only individuals or smaller communities, while in politics and science it is only used as propaganda or in a similarly rhetorical way.

In September 1945, Albert Einstein and Thomas Mann, along with some American journalists and scientists, composed a declaration:

> The first atom bomb has not only destroyed the city of Hiroshima; it has also finally annihilated our traditional political ideas, which have long been out of date . . . The existence of our civilization depends on whether we cultivate the science of humane relationships: the capacity of people of the most different kinds to live together and work together in peace in the same world.

Since then thousands upon thousands of scintillating, humane writings have appeared. But at the same time hundreds and thousands of increasingly new, increasingly more effective atom bombs have been produced, and other means of mass destruction have been devised.

What should govern world politics in the future

Between 1958 and 1963, Andrei Sakharov attempted in vain to explain to Kruschchev's government that further nuclear tests were extremely dangerous for human beings and nature. Kruschchev retorted: 'Sakharov must not give us lessons in politics. Scientists should mind their own business; questions of armament are a matter of state politics.'

Even before the fall of Kruschchev, he and his minister succeeded in banishing nuclear tests underground, with the creation of international agreements to this effect. In July 1968, in his memorandum 'Reflections on progress, peaceful co-existence and intellectual freedom', Sakharov explained the need to support state policy both scientifically and morally.

However, soon after that Soviet tanks destroyed Czech 'socialism with a human face', and in the following decades bloody wars have been raging in Afghanistan and Nicaragua, in South East Asia, in the Persian Gulf, in South Africa, in Lebanon, in Abkhazia, Chechenia, Tadjikistan, in the Kurdish areas of Turkey and in Iran. Ever new terrorist bombs are being detonated, and on general staffs, learned soldiers are outlining detailed plans for new great wars on earth and in the cosmos; while scientists all over the world who are faithful to their callings and obedient to their governments are developing ever more perfect means of exterminating human beings and destroying the environment.

In March 1981, in the second year of his exile, Andrei Sakharov succeeded in passing on to his friends an appeal entitled 'The Responsibility of Scientists':

> In today's world, through the international character of science, scientists are creating what is for the moment the only international community which really exists. But the integration of this community is inexorably leading to a still higher level . . . to a broad group which covers moral and universally human problems.

In this appeal he called on his colleagues throughout the world to be aware that their knowledge, their scientific and technological achievements and experiences, brought not only beneficent progress to civilization, but also the utmost dangers for humankind.

Today, after Hiroshima and Chernobyl, human beings are living in a highly endangered world, on the banks and shores of poisoned rivers and lakes, in cities which are throttled by smog and traffic, in countries which are threatened with catastrophic over-population and mass death by famine. Therefore it is not enough for governments now and then to allow themselves to be advised by scientists: not only the natural sciences but also the humanities – with as little ideology as possible – must become the foundation of state politics.

What may we, what should we now conclude on the topic of a global ethic? Is it, as it always was, a fine utopia, a daydream of men of good will, who always everywhere were in the minority? Today that is still the case. But tomorrow and the day after, the imperishable dreams of humanity and justice, the most recent Declaration of the Parliament of the World's Religions, should become a policy for the whole world. For leading statesmen, politicians, businessmen, scientists, journalists, entrepreneurs, for all those who control weapons and the media, they must become guiding principles, the criteria and aims of their activity.

Unless that happens, unless the old and new daydreams of a global ethic become an everyday reality in the spiritual and social life of all peoples, then either in a few years all living creatures will be destroyed by nuclear catastrophes, by poison gases used in war, or by pestilences directed by science, or before many centuries are past all human beings, animals and plants will die a tormenting death on polluted soil, in poisoned rivers and lakes in a damaged atmosphere. There are no other prospects.

We should not wait and hope for any revelation. Unless we ourselves learn from our experiences to obliterate hostile images and 'ancestral enmities' in order to achieve peaceful relations and a lasting understanding between the different nations, religions, forms of state and ideologies, then both the 'house of Europe' and soon afterwards the whole planet will become uninhabitable.

A global ethic is urgently necessary.

No Human Progress without a Global Ethic

MARY ROBINSON

The author is President of the Republic of Ireland

The fiftieth anniversary of the United Nations provides a timely focus, and a chastening reminder of how far away we are from achieving the vision of its Preamble, beginning 'We the Peoples . . .'

The imbalance between power and powerlessness

The sad truth is that we have not developed that vital sense of connectedness, that shared ethic on which we could go forward together. I join with those, including the representatives of the Parliament of the World's Religions which drew up this Declaration, who believe it is of fundamental importance that we renew our commitment in the direction of an ethic which can be shared and supported by all nations, cultures and religions: a universal ethic as the basis for human rights, human reponsibilities and human connectedness.

Not the least of the importances of a global ethic is that the very search for it must draw together a great variety of men and women, of different heritages, cultures, religions and convictions. This guarantees that a global ethic, from the very beginning, must be a process rather than simply a product: that it must mirror the diversity it seeks to address. Anything else would result in a static series of orthodox opinions of which there are far too many already. The search for it, therefore, with all the debate and difference inherent in that quest, must be undertaken patiently and without pre-existing assumptions. At the same time the search for it requires the determination on all sides that it can and will be found, simply because its absence at the moment imperils human progress.

Perhaps, therefore, before deciding on the substantive basis of the ethic itself, we need to define those forces in the contemporary world which could befriend the search for it; whose use for such a purpose would ennoble the means. There is, to start with, the new technology. Cyberspace has not only made neighbours of us all; it also stands itself in urgent need of ethical definition. It is at the moment a neutral resource. But the truth is that it should be able to offer the same access to the powerless as to the powerful. The use of such an enormous resource to connect men and women across their differences, and through a method which emphasizes their equality, achieves two ends. It puts us in touch with one another. But it also, and more importantly, harnesses a resource of naked power on the side of those who are vulnerable to isolation and powerlessness, offering them the possibility of the same opportunities for expression as those who are powerful.

It is this imbalance between power and powerlessness which is at the heart of the search for a global ethic. Therefore we need to identify ways of correcting the imbalance. To start with we need to see our connectedness to one another, which has itself become, in today's world, a moral choice. On recent state visits to several African countries I was particularly struck by their sense of isolation, by their feeling that they had slipped from the European agenda. And behind that, it seems to me, is the entire and almost hidden drama of how their plight is presented to the rest of the world. The culture of the news image and the brief sound-bite, far from emphasizing that connectedness I speak of, invites us to disown it; invites us, in fact, to relegate to visual images and forgettable news stories the complex suffering of men and women to whom we are in fact deeply connected by both humanity and obligation.

Any global ethic must seek, as a matter of urgency, to restore that connectedness.

Listening – sharing – participation

One of the chief ways of doing this is by listening. We must find the ability to listen to the narrative of each other's diversities, so that we can draw strength and not weakness from our differences. At the moment it is hard to distinguish those differences which are true differences from those divisions which come simply from a lack of listening to one another. To enable the true adherent of the Islamic faith to listen with respect to the equally true follower of the Christian faith – and to be listened to in turn – to encourage a genuine dialogue between the Judaic and Muslim heritages, Hindu and Buddhist, must be a chief object of a global ethic.

Central also to any global ethic is the concept of sharing, which would have to mean tackling with honesty and seriousness of purpose the huge inequity of resources between peoples and nations in different parts of the world. Let us not be too abstract in our approach. A starting point could be to reflect on the reality of the millions of children who lack access to safe water. What if it was your child or mine? We need a concept of sharing which moves beyond the old model of development aid to radical rethinking, leading to fundamental structural change.

Finally, the true foundation of any global ethic lies in the principle of participation. Ironically, it is one of the achievements of political thinking in this century to have realized how vital this principle is to the survival of democracies and the well-being of nation states. Yet, as we move towards the end of the century, we have not found the methods which guarantee adequate participation of all the people in those structures which vitally affect their well-being and the future of their children. Yet the lack of this causes those very cynicisms, alienations and disaffections which threaten modern societies.

Perhaps here we see an immediate challenge to women in positions of leadership to contribute ideas and approaches which deepen that participation. I have been struck by the open, participatory, enabling, supportive structures adopted quite naturally by women's groups and networks – interestingly a trend evident throughout the world, North and South, developed and developing – which could offer innovative and challenging approaches to sharing power rather than wielding it.

What is clear is that for the first time ever the pursuit of a goal by humanity, the attempt to move in the direction of a minimal consensus of shared values, attitudes and moral standards, will require the same degree of commitment and equal contribution of women and men.

Key Principles for a Humane Society

HELMUT SCHMIDT

From 1974 to 1982 the author was Chancellor of the Federal Republic of Germany. He is editor of Die Zeit

Among the particularly good memories of my time as Chancellor of the Federal Republic of Germany is a whole series of personal relationships with people who had similar responsibilities.

Reflecting again on ethical principles

Some of these close and confidential partnerships became friendships which often transcended very different origins and national interests. One that was particularly important to me was the warm and very personal friendship which I had with Anwar el Sadat, the Egyptian President, who was murdered in 1981. He was an earnest and pious Muslim, and we often discussed religious questions. As we did so, we spoke of the possibilities of faith, and of building bridges of reconciliation, understanding and peace. President Sadat kept coming back to one idea: a meeting of the top representatives of the Jewish, Christian and Islamic faith communities on Mount Sinai, the place where Jews, Christians and Muslims all believe that God's commandment was given to men. We talked about what shared prayer, shared reflection on what we have in common in matters of faith and ethics, at this place could mean for the divided region of the Middle East and far beyond.

These wishes, which were almost dreams, came to my mind as I read the Declaration on a Global Ethic which emerged from a meeting of representatives of so many and at first sight such different religious and faith communities. What had seemed to us in Egypt at that time so daring, almost a distant utopia, for the religions of Judaism, Christianity and Islam, which are so related in their roots and their concept of God, has become possible in this document from the Parliament of the World's Religions on the basis of far greater differences in views of the world and God between religions of very different character. It is to be wondered at that this has become possible out of an awareness that human beings have an unavoidable responsibility for the whole earth and today face an urgent need to find a comprehensive and global order for its society.

The document presented here rightly sees the way to a remedy in renewed reflection on universally binding ethical principles. It rightly recalls that hitherto ethical principles relevant to society have always grown from religious sources and have gained their force and binding quality as a religious duty. It is impressive to see how quite manifest agreements on the central questions of life and society have emerged from a bold dialogue which has transcended so many frontiers, and how such realistic criteria and basic attitudes have been worked out.

In March 1987, under the joint direction of my Japanese friend Takeo Fukuda and myself, a discussion was held at the Civiltà Cattolica in Rome on peace, development, population and the environment between members of the Inter-Action Council and spiritual leaders of the most important world religions: a Buddhist, a Muslim, a Methodist, a Protestant, a Roman Catholic cardinal, a Hindu, a Jew and a freethinker. The representatives on the political side came from dictatorships and democracies of different stamps: conservatives, liberals and communists, with black, brown, yellow and white skins. Despite the difference and opposition between the perspectives of the religious representatives and the politicians, an astonishing degree of agreement was arrived at over the fundamental difficulties in the world. We agreed that 'humankind is confronted with its most far-reaching crises in history without having defined or thought out measures appropriate for tackling them . . . ', and that grappling with the problems would produce 'many fields of collaboration between spiritual and political leaders in shared commitment to moral values, peace and human prosperity'.

Do the religions have the power?

But do the religions today have the power to communicate a binding ethic? In the conditions of modern civilization, are they in a position to shape human behaviour comprehensively? Has not their influence long been limited to more or less tiny minorities, who are confronted with a secularized lifestyle among the majority which has long left traditional ties behind?

The questions oppress me as I consider the situation in the Christian cultures of the West. Here people do not even seem to be aware how our ideas of human and civil rights are rooted in an ethic which once had a religious stamp.

I am not presenting these questions as a counter-argument. Rather, I want to point out that the dialogue towards a global ethic and its acceptance among the religions must aim at a further step, namely also to make itself understood in the secularized spheres of our society. The key principles for human life and society which are worked out here offer a good basis for this dialogue.

During my time as Chancellor, in a speech on basic values in state and society I observed that the state itself cannot create the values and moral foundations on which the democratic state is inevitably dependent. I remarked: 'The free state, the ideologically neutral, democratic state, lives by values which existed before it. It did not create them, and it cannot guarantee their continued existence without putting its freedom in question. Rather, it finds them in individuals and in society, and it must relate its action to where they are alive.'

What I said at that time about the modern state with a democratic constitution applies in a transferred sense to our modern societies as well. Our life is shaped by the fact that in some areas of society, traditions and obligations are being kept alive which were historically influential on the culture and values of the whole of society. There can no longer be a uniform ethic; it must grow out of the living values of individuals and groups.

I am grateful that a Parliament of the World's Religions has taken a first step towards undertaking this discussion of a global ethic.

Shared International Responsibility

MARTTI AHTISAARI

The author is President of the Republic of Finland

The declaration approved by the Parliament of the World's Religions at its Chicago Conference on 5 September 1993 is a welcome step towards a deepening of the awareness of a shared international responsibility. The Declaration is not only addressed to the members of the world religions, but is also meant to stimulate discussion among political leaders and representatives of the world's governments. How do the principles of the Declaration relate to the international aims which Finland has pursued in recent decades?

A global ethic promotes the aims of the Conference on Security and Co-operation in Europe

Both scholars and politicians have emphasized how significant the Conference on Security and Co-operation in Europe (CSCE), the 'Helsinki Process', proved for the changes in Eastern Europe. Finland, the host country of the Helsinki conference, played an important role in the initial phase of the new Europe. Human rights questions, which became the focus of international discussion with the 'third basket' of the CSCE, had a significant share in the collapse of the old political and social constellation.

Three dimensions can be identified in the Helsinki process in which the process brought about actual changes. All of them had great significance for the implementation of human rights.

First, the Helsinki Conference instituted a permanent dialogue on the basic rights of the individual which forced even the Eastern people's democracies to take this question seriously.

Secondly, the Helsinki Conference elevated violations of human rights to the status of international questions which allowed the 'intervention' of other states.

And thirdly, the Helsinki Conference can be credited with having helped to establish universally the view that human rights and security are indivisible. This in turn has made it easier for human rights movements to be active, especially in the socialist countries.

In the meantime it has proved possible to implement many of the human rights which are called for, though in many places economic problems threaten their credibility. Rights which are not coupled with duties easily lead to a situation in which the right of the stronger prevails. On the other hand, duties are easily abused if they are not backed up by an ethical world view. A new and juster political order in Europe is not possible without the power which grows from a new basic ethical attitude which has been chosen freely. In this connection we can also establish from our limited European perspective that a new world order cannot come into being without a new ethical order. This is also noted in the Declaration of the Parliament of the World's Religions. By creating a new ethical world order, the Chicago Declaration is helping to create a new and juster world order.

Cultural and ethical values

In attempts over recent decades to achieve a state of sustained development, there has been an emphasis on the importance of the economic components. For a whole series of reasons, the programme of the 1970s to establish a just economic order (the new economic order) in the world has run out of steam. Now is the time to understand the significance of education and environmental awareness as factors for the development of our culture.

The age of political and economic systems is measured in decades or centuries; by contrast, the religions and ethical systems which underlie culture are millennia old. It makes sense to base the development of thought and culture on those values which have proved most lasting, by orientating international and national aims on them. So it is important to reflect on the basic values which underlie cultures, which have global validity and sustain life. I am firmly convinced that a more lasting culture can be created on this basis. It would offer the best foundation for the creation of a sustained development which would benefit humankind and ensure an ecological equilibrium.

Information as an ethical problem

The media bear great responsibility in the creation of a new, international order with a more durable ethic and of the cultural climate which this needs. The freedom of the media must not be restricted, but at the same time the media have to recognize their ethical responsibility.

From the perspective of global responsibility it is important for the media, in their reporting, to accord due status to those topics and events which promote the general good of the world. It is also essential to be able to rely on the information disseminated by the media, especially in situations of crisis. There are instances when the clergy of a place have been the only authority which could consistently shape the social conscience in difficult political and social conflicts. Namibia in the 1970s is one instance of this.

The Chicago Declaration provides a useful foundation for the debate on ethics and values. Beyond question it can serve to revive ethical awareness, but above all it is an invitation to the different levels of the world's population to reflect on what we can do to fulfil our responsibility to influence global development in a positive, ethically acceptable way.

Indispensable for Survival

CORNELIO SOMMARUGA

*The author is President of the International Committee
of the Red Cross in Geneva*

I would like to offer some personal comments on the extremely interesting Declaration on a Global Ethic which was adopted in Chicago on 4 September 1993 by the Parliament of the World's Religions and has now been published by you.

In accord with the principles of the Red Cross

This Declaration contains principles which in essentials correspond with the humanitarian principles which the International Committee of the Red Cross has always defended actively and in law since its creation in 1863.

1995 is not only the fiftieth anniversary of the United Nations Organization but also the thirtieth anniversary of the proclamation of the Principles of the Red Cross and the Red Crescent by the International Conference of the Red Cross, which met in Vienna in 1965. I would like to quote these seven principles and comment on them briefly here:

Humanity: The concept of humanity can be found in all religions, all traditions, all civilizations, all philosophical movements. As the Declaration emphasizes, it is essential today to understand that all of humanity is a single family, no matter to what religion, tradition, civilization or philosophy it belongs.

Impartiality: Impartiality is both the recognition of the equality of men and women, the demand for equitable benefits according to needs, and an impartial attitude without preconceptions and prejudices.

Neutrality: Abstention from participation in political, racial, religious or ideological controversies makes it possible to keep the trust of all, recognizing only suffering human beings who deserve help and protection, without discrimination.

Independence: Any self-respecting humanitarian action must be independent at a political, confessional and economic level.

Voluntariness: This principle expresses the deliberate and disinterested character of humanitarian action.

Unity: Unity is both cohesion and harmony, and the openness of the national societies, without any discrimination, in their recruitment of members and collaborators, who must be prepared to be active throughout the whole territory.

Universality: Humanity knows no frontiers; it must triumph everywhere and always.

Towards the respecting of human dignity

In the present world situation of violence and conflict it is vital that organizations of all kinds should reaffirm, endorse, make known and apply the values of respect for humanity, life and peace, even if formulations and approaches may differ. The International Committee of the Red Cross is not a religious organization, but it welcomes all those voices which, each in their domain and by their own channels, seek to prevent further violence, suffering and destruction.

All political and military authorities and all peoples must be convinced of the need to respect the life and dignity of every human being in all circumstances.

From this perspective, I am persuaded that the notions of the interdependence of the rights of all human beings, of solidarity, and of commitment on behalf of humanity in tolerance and non-violence are an integral part of a cause common to the whole of humanity, of an ethical strategy which is indispensable for its survival.

So I would like to offer my congratulations on this Declaration on a Global Ethic and express my hope that it will become known throughout the world.

An Inspiration for All of Us

JUAN SOMAVIA

The Author is Chilean Ambassador at the United Nations and was President of the UN Social Summit in Copenhagen in 1995

I heartily endorse this Declaration – and with it, the statement of principles and accompanying framework for a global ethic so beautifully elaborated.

The transforming power of the ethic

I uphold the abiding values expressed herein, most especially the belief that all people should strive to reject domination and violence and should embrace our interdependence – not fear it.

I, too, encourage patience, acceptance and generosity as among the most noble human qualities to encourage in each and every individual. Hand in hand with them comes the natural rejection of intolerance and injustice – especially hatred and violence falsely 'justified' in the name of religion.

As so convincingly expressed in this Declaration, the central principles of religious teachings constitute a common corpus of abiding values for a world ethic. The ancient criteria of human behaviour can and must form the basis for a just and enduring world order. Religious believers can indeed extend these principles openly to other individuals – neither judgmentally nor with a sense of obligation but rather in faith, secure in the hope that the radically transforming power of this ethic will open new horizons for the future well-being of all people and of our planet.

True, a global ethic cannot offer pat solutions to the immense problems confronting humanity; rather, it constitutes the moral reservoir from which women and men draw the strength to liberate ourselves, individually and collectively, from the powerful forces which oppress us. It inspires a vision of peaceful living and shared responsibility which transcends the potential divisiveness of politics, race, ethnicity, gender – indeed, of religion itself.

I take from this Declaration the vision of a banner into which religious believers of all stripes can weave their hopes, dreams and ideals. The banner, and the ethical message it conveys, embroiders the basic precepts of the Universal Declaration of Human Rights, securing them with a holistic respect for the human person, the inalienable character of liberty, and the fundamental equality and interdependence of all human beings. It incorporates the many threads of the Declaration and Programme of Action of the World Summit for Social Development – inspired, as these documents are, by the vibrant expression of civil society, worldwide.

Putting principles into practice

For if we have learned anything from personally observing the precarious history of our planet, we know that true commitment to rights and liberty presupposes an individual consciousness of our responsibilities and obligations to one another, something that must mediate between our heads and our hearts. As this Declaration so correctly states, rights without ethics are not long for this world – and cannot form the basis for a new world order.

Nor can the inviolable and inalienable dignity of the human person be safeguarded and guaranteed without commitment in word as well as deed to a core set of ancient and yet utterly contemporary principles – principles held fast by religious people worldwide. As so well elaborated in this Declaration, these include: 1. non-violence and respect for human life;

2. social solidarity and a just economic order; 3. a culture of tolerance, honesty and truth; and 4. equality and comraderie among women and men.

For these principles to infuse all of our social and economic institutions – our corporations, media and outlets of scientific inquiry among them – each person will need to arouse within themselves the will to translate principle into practice, ideas into action, personal commitment into community living. I uphold with you this Declaration, as a guiding inspiration for each of us to embrace in the movement together 'Toward a Global Ethic'.

My Irrevocable Creed

RIGOBERTA MENCHU

The author is a champion of the civil rights of the Indios in Guatemala. She has been awarded the Nobel Peace Prize

Instead of a direct commentary on the Declaration on a Global Ethic, Rigoberta Menchu put at our disposal the following 'General Principles of Conduct for the 1992 Nobel Peace Prize Recipient', which is an expressive statement of her ethical creed

Indispensable ingredients of peace

I. Commitment to struggle for peace:
   Peace is not only the end of conflicts; it is also the expression of economic development with social justice.
   Peace must guarantee relations of equality and mutual respect between northern and southern countries.
   Peace must include above all complete respect for human rights, sovereignty and self-determination.
   Peace must include respect for cultural differences, the equality of people and cultures. Respect for diversity is the basis of living together in harmony.
   The establishment of peace must guarantee the rights of displaced populations and refugees from the world's conflicts.

II. Commitment to New Ethics:
   The firm defence of the points elaborated above are the basis of a new ethical proposal.

This gives predominance to respect for collective values
over individualism, solidarity over indifference, respect
for nature over its general depredation.
This new ethical proposal is opposed to all forms of
corruption and all manifestations of racism.
Above all, it cultivates hope for a better future for all of
humanity. All of this ethical planning must be accompanied by an integral education.
It is indispensible that the means of social communication be strengthened with this activity and that they be
involved in this commitment to a new ethics.

III. Commitment to struggle for the International Decade of
Indigenous Peoples and a Universal Declaration Concerning Indigenous Peoples and First Nations:

That indigenous peoples and first nations participate in
all those decisions which have to do with building their
future.

IV. The reaffirmation of support for the struggles of poor and
oppressed peoples for their liberation and for the social
transformation necessary to build a future based on social
justice.

V. The above-stated principles have been established in the
struggle for liberty, equality, fraternity; the respect for
cultural diversity, human rights, sovereignty and self-determination.

All of these are the indispensable ingredients of peace.
They must be a type of permanent and irrevocable creed.

Commitment for Guatemala

1. The political solution to the conflict is the path to
building peace in the country. In the present situation of

the negotiation process, it has become necessary to urge the reinitiation of negotiations, to defend the accords reached in Oslo together with the sectors of the society which demanded them, and to endorse the participation of Monseignor Rodolfo Quezada Toruho as conciliator.

2. Defend the right of refugees to return to their country, in a collective, organized and voluntary manner, with a verifiable guarantee for personal integrity. Further, this should be accompanied by meeting the demands of those displaced within the country.

   Urge the establishment of a petition in mutual agreement with the refugees with the goal of their return.

3. Human Rights. Demand their enforcement and complete fulfilment and the immediate end of impunity. Demand the fulfilment of the recommendations of Mr Christian Tomoushat (United Nations expert) and support the demands of the groups that came into being because of violence and impunity.

4. It is necessary to rationalize the use and the occupation of land as a right of the majority of the peasant and indigenous population, as an urgent matter for social development.

   Definitively support the demands of those groups involved in the struggle for the rationalization of the use and the occupation of land.

5. The state and private workers must have the right to a free organization without conditions. Better wages, working conditions and free organization are inseparable.

6. Promote the struggle for the rights of indigenous peoples:

   (a) Work together with those present and future efforts for the strengthening of Mayan unity and consensus;

   (b) Push for a National Indigenous Summit Meeting. This should include content for the Decade of Indigenous Peoples.

   (c) Back the Mayan proposals regarding petitions, consensus and civil co-ordinators such as the National Petitions of Consensus, the Multisectorial Social Forum, Co-ordinators of Civil Sectors and Civil Co-ordinators for Peace.

(d) Support and strengthen every force, organization and struggle for the defence and recognition of indigenous peoples' rights.

(e) Support and strengthen the signing and the ratification of the agreements regarding Indigenous Peoples' Rights; support local legal initiatives which seek to improve the material and spiritual situation of indigenous peoples.

7. In the present occasion, demand, as the Multisectorial Social Forum and the National Petition of Consensus have done, the purging of state organisms involved in *coups d'état*, corruption and repression.

Without this necessary purging, one cannot think of a real and truly institutionalized democracy, nor of overcoming the vices of the previous regimes.

Public ethics and morals depend on an integral education which considers the recovery of the values of the family and the community, in addition to an effective purging.

8. Struggle as a long term objective for national unity, taking up, giving life and body to what is contained in the Declaration of Kaminal Juyu (21 December 1982).

9. Demand the democratization and autonomy of municipal power, as well as strengthening other forms of neighbourhood and community organization, and the different forms of organization and expression of indigenous peoples.

10. Support and strengthen all of the local, regional and national forces which favour the predominance of civil society over any form of military, authoritarian or political imposition which violates human rights. In other words, struggle for the demilitarization of the society.

11. Promulgate an integral education for peace, human rights, Mayan rights, democracy and development in close harmony with nature. That this be done beginning in the place where one lives, works or studies. And that it develop in a participatory manner founded on solidarity.

12. Strengthen the struggle for freedom of expression as a full part of human rights.

The Declaration on a Global Ethic

CARL FRIEDRICH VON WEIZSÄCKER

The author, who is a physicist and philosopher, has been awarded the Peace Prize of the German Book Trade

The Parliament of the World's Religions, in Chicago 1993, made a Declaration on a Global Ethic. The authors of the present volume have been invited to comment on this on the basis of their own personal convictions and experience. I shall attempt to do this from three perspectives:
– scientific experience,
– the role of ethics in religion,
– the inner experience of the religions which has been handed on and is still to come.

Scientific experience

The natural sciences are nowadays usually thought to be value-free, because they are science. That twice two is four, that the planets move round the sun in accordance with mechanical laws, that according to our present knowledge matter consists of atoms which obey the laws of quantum theory, that the human brain consists of nerves which are linked effectively with one another and with the other organs of the body, will be acknowledged by all who have understood it, regardless of what they desire or what ethical or religious belief they follow. That is an experience. On my travels in North and South America, in India, East Asia and Africa, I have come to know a great variety of cultures and value systems, but as a physicist I have immediately been in agreement with the physicists there about the statements of physics.

This concept of value freedom was coined in the nineteenth century as a formula to protect the recognition of scientific truths against the demands of the prevailing political or religious creeds. But the recognition of this independence of science from value is itself experienced as a great social value, as a doctrine of the freedom of human beings in dealing with one another.

But if value-free science is itself a value, then evidently science, too, comes under certain ethical criteria. The content of the scientific statements given as examples above is valid independently of our values. But that we do science at all is a human decision which is here regarded as a value. Is that always the case? Nowadays there is a good deal of scepticism on this point. May I split the nucleus of the atom or engage in gene technology out of scientific curiosity?

As a first example I have chosen a science which already in antiquity was developed for its effect on human beings: medicine. Right from antiquity the physician has been required to take the Hippocratic oath: 'I will use my knowledge only for the well-being of my fellow men, not to their detriment and never to their death.' This oath was also a protection against unethical demands on a physician from political or economic powers: 'I may not do what you ask of me here. I have sworn an oath.' In our century, physics and chemistry have become sources of such great power that the question has arisen whether every natural scientist should not swear a Hippocratic oath.

But here as always, when one takes ethics seriously, the question of detail arises. Here, I shall again begin with medicine as an example. At least in Germany, in recent years the question of medical ethics has become a very live one. Now there are chairs for ethics, and joint medical-ethical commissions. But the difficulty emerges precisely in the discussions of such commissons. Those who have taken part in them have occasionally painted the following picture. The medical representatives on the commission say: 'If action by a doctor is medically right, then it is automatically also the right action ethically.' The ethical representatives think, and probably also say: 'We know what is ethically right; the principles of ethics tell us that. So we do not need to study medical detail.' The consequence is a confrontation between two intransigent standpoints. In truth the doctor must not think only of the immediate causal consequences of his actions. The doctor must learn to understand patients as individuals, and detect the biographical and psycho-somatic links. 'The body is often wiser than the consciousness', said Viktor von Weizsäcker in his *Anthropologische Medizin*. And ethics does not just call for norms. It calls for perception of the fellow human being, the effect of love of the neighbour. Doctors have to learn to perceive themselves, to understand and criticize themselves, in particular in their spontaneous reactions. This is a wide field, and I leave it to the reader's judgment.

To turn to my own discipline, physics. In 1932 Chadwick discovered the neutron. My teacher Werner Heisenberg immediately concluded that now it was possible to state that the nucleus of the atom was made up of protons and neutrons. This led me in my twenties to chose nuclear physics as my sphere of work. In December 1938 Otto Hahn discovered uranium fission. In February or March 1939, about 200 professional nuclear physicists all over the world knew that now it would be possible to make atom bombs. The day I understood that, I went to my friend Georg Picht to discuss the consequences. We drew three conclusions:

1. If atom bombs are possible, someone will build them.
2. If atom bombs are built, someone will use them.
3. In that case, in the long run humankind has only two options: to destroy itself or to abolish war as an institution.

The first two conclusions were very soon confirmed: in 1945 the bombs fell on Hiroshima and Nagasaki. The third conclusion still confronts us as a question. So I must speak of it here.

For millennia, the legal institutions within a state have

contained a prohibition against killing a fellow citizen; only the state authorities may kill, as a defence against crime and as a death penalty. Now war is an institution recognized by international law. From that very fact we can draw two conclusions: by international law the building and use of such weapons was not forbidden, and as people feared the weapons in the hands of their political opponents, they felt justified, indeed compelled, to make such weapons themselves and, if need be, to use them.

What ethical conclusions follow?

Individual physicists could dissociate themselves from taking part in the development of nuclear weapons. In so doing they would then remain morally pure. But this would not be of much help towards saving humankind from these weapons. Could such people hope to persuade all the physicists in the world? Could they do so in the Second World War which was just beginning, or later in the 'Cold War' between the great powers, in the threat of an armed North-South conflict?

The states attempted to prevent the further spread of these weapons in the Nuclear Weapons Proliferation Treaty of 1968. Those who already had such weapons announced negotiations for dismantling them, though since then they have not in fact made much progress; those who had no nuclear weapons were explicitly to renounce having them. In 1969 an Indian colleague said to me: 'We Indians are not signing the treaty. We Indians are followers of Mahatma Gandhi. Can we sign a treaty which implies that we are morally unworthy to possess such weapons while a power which has already killed several hundred thousand Japanese with these weapons is said to be morally worthy to possess them?' Since then nuclear weapons have not been used again in war. But for how long can we count that they will not be? And new scientific inventions, chemical and biological weapons, world-wide television propaganda, and so on are emerging. In an age of scientific technology, how are we to distinguish in the long term between weapons which are allowed and weapons which are banned? Humankind senses that the institution of war must be superseded.

Weapons of war are not the only problem for a technological age. In addition to peace among human beings there is the requirement of peace with nature. Ecology is becoming an urgent problem all over the world. The climatic catastrophe which threatens is one example.

I am convinced that all this is the ethical concern of all natural scientists. Many in our discipline argue that we are only engaged in value-free research, and that its consequences are a matter for politicians. But how can wise and responsible politicians act reasonably when they know in advance that they will lose the next election just because they have acted reasonably? And how can they avoid losing the election if public opinion is not educated, seriously and on matters of principle? And who is to teach public opinion if even the specialists want to get out of their own obligation to teach? If parents show their three-year-old how to light a match, go for a walk and come back to find their house in flames, who is to blame – the child or the parents?

But how is a generally recognized, knowledgeable and effective ethic possible?

The role of ethics in religion

The Declaration on a Global Ethic is addressed to all the religions on earth, and also to ethics with no religious basis. It calls on them to discover, state and follow ethical principles which are common to them all.

First let us look at the foundation of ethics in religion, which is historically prior. How does religion present itself in human history? I once attempted to distinguish four aspects of religion. Religon emerges as
(*a*) the vehicle of a culture,

(*b*) radical ethics,
(*c*) inner experience,
(*d*) theology.

As the vehicle of a culture, religion shapes social life, organizes time, defines or justifies morality, interprets anxieties, provides forms of expression for joys, comforts the helpless and interprets the world. In this role it preserves, it is conservative. But this description of its role comes after the event. A religion which is fully alive knows the effect it has, but for the religion this effect is the consequence of the divine reality in the present. Thus its ethical precepts are not explained. Anyone who asks how they are justified is already affected by doubt.

Historically, the way in which the three other aspects have been consciously worked out is in itself already an answer to doubt. Radical ethics usually presents itself as God's commandment or as the requirement of reason. Inner experience, as prayer, mediation, revelation, points to the origin of religious faith. Today we mostly use theology – a word which comes from Greek philosophy – to describe the attempt of religion to understand itself rationally.

Where a global ethic is concerned, the rationality of the Enlightenment becomes the indispensable partner of the religions. The religions have to recognize their differences and work them out clearly, and precisely in so doing learn together to find, identify and call for the ethical foundations which they have in common.

Historically, the conviction that there are ethical foundations common to all human beings has often been expressed in new religions. However, usually this has soon been denied them by the other religions which preceded them in history. In particular the Western, 'prophetic' religions of Judaism, Christianity and Islam have tended towards intolerance. Only in the recent centuries of modernity in the West have we gradually learned to know the great religions outside our sphere, in personal dealings with their representatives, and to take them seriously. If we explain the Enlightenment in terms of belief in scientific thought, we could regard the Enlightenment as the only religion which is a world-wide faith today. The term 'religion' is not usually used for the Enlightenment. But we must remember that at least historically the Enlightenment is a child of Greek philosophy, and in the Roman empire that in turn was *de facto* the common religion of the educated, and therefore penetrated deeply into Christian theology. So the Declaration on a Global Ethic is right in also turning to ethics which are not grounded in any of the existing religions.

Now what is the ethic shared by the religions and the Enlightenment? The Golden Rule gives the first answer: 'Do not do to others what you would not want them to do to you', or, in a positive form, 'Treat others as you would want them to treat you.' Kant, who defined the Enlightenment as 'mankind's emergence from a tutelage which it brought on itself', framed the rule in the categorical imperative: 'Act in such a way that the maxims of your action can always be the principle of a universal legislation.' If reason thinks in universal terms, the Golden Rule is the principle of ethical reason.

But the examples from the natural sciences have already shown us that ethics has to go into detail. How have the religions done that? Here the many differences of customs, norms and rituals are immediately obvious. This is the real sphere in which the Declaration on a Global Ethic is a call for work. Seek in and behind the differences that which nevertheless you all find convincing! And measure it by the human needs which can be recognized today, like peace among humankind and peace between humankind and nature! In the Western religions these demands appear in the Ten Commandments, and, by way of clarification, in Jesus' Sermon on the Mount.

I hope that here once again I may use my own personal experiences as an example. These are experiences from my childhood. Children are often more spontaneously sensitive than adults, who have to wrap themselves up in complications. When I was twelve I began to read the New Testament and immediately came upon the Sermon on the Mount. This shook me deeply: 'This is manifest truth, yet none of us does it.' Today, as an old man, I would say: 'It is simple reason, even if some phrases are put in time-conditioned language.' However, when I was around fourteen and saw the religious differences among my fellow pupils as I do so now among all humankind, I had to say: 'Would the good God have caused me in particular to be born into the only true religion? I must take all religions seriously.' That was a lifelong task. But the ethic of the Sermon on the Mount remained evident truth. Where I violated this truth – and how often I have done so! – I was aware that I too was a sinner and needed self-criticism and inner help.

What is inner help? We can distinguish three levels in the Sermon on the Mount. It is first of all a commandment to act handed down in the Torah, the Jewish Law, and here presented in a heightened form. It is then a commandment about our inner disposition, of the kind that can also already be found in the prophets. And right at the beginning of the text it is the truth of the Beatitudes. The Beatitudes express inner experience. In their deepest roots, not only the ethic, but also the inner experience are common to the religions. But most religions no longer express these common features.

Incomplete religion

If we want to discover a global ethic as a necessary condition for the solution of the practical problems of individuals and societies today, we will have to seek the agreement of the religions on profound ethical principles and an expression of that agreement. However, while this condition is indeed necessary, it is not sufficient, in two respects.

First, much detailed specialist work is very difficult. I remarked on that earlier. And this work does not get anywhere unless there is at least a hint of agreement in principle. To try to formulate this agreement in a way which is free from contradiction is difficult, and is perhaps unnecessary right at the beginning of the work, but we are inexorably required to seek it.

Secondly, in seeking to state principles, we cannot avoid reflecting on inner experience. The quest for a global ethic will necessarily throw those in search of the truth back on their inner experience. And that is not just the ethical experience expressed in the Beatitudes. On a concrete level it is at the same time prayer, the liturgy as shared prayer, and meditation. Liturgies and therefore inward prayers which can be formulated differ. The way to meditation is described in words which presuppose a particular theology. And theologies are profoundly different. In a writing dedicated to the Dalai Lama, the Protestant Bishop Krusche of Hamburg relates how the Dalai Lama said to him: 'We should not conceal the differences. For example, we Buddhists do not believe in a creator God as you Christians do.' Be this as it may, an encounter between the leading experiences of the cultures of the world is inescapable. The Western Enlightenment has conquered Asia; it dominates technocratic Japan, Communist China, and India as a representative democracy and growing economy – all of them, with all their problems. But thinking people in the West often long for the meditative experience of the East. Esoteric sects often have stronger wills than the churches, the membership of which is constantly decreasing.

So we are directed towards the experience of history. Human history is an incomplete advance over the very short period of a few millennia. Where it is leading is uncertain. Total catastrophe is possible, as we see today more clearly than ever before. A completion has increasingly been dreamed of.

Religion is incomplete. The Enlightenment is incomplete. Religion today can take the next necessary step only if it is quite serious about the Enlightenment. The Enlightenment can take the next necessary step only if it is quite serious about religion.

In view of this, how can we treat the differences in ethical norms, the pointers towards inner experiences, and the theologies which interpret both of these? At the beginning of work on the project of a global ethic, for good pragmatic reasons the differences are first being allowed to stand, in a spirit of tolerance.

But tolerance is not the permanent solution. When there is tolerance, two different legitimate principles are often allowed to stand without differentiation. Co-humanity is essentially tolerant of actual dealings between human beings; indeed, it loves difference as an expression of the richness of humanity. No two people are the same, nor should they be; no two cultures are the same, nor should they be. But recognized truth is essentially intolerant of recognized error. It can tolerate the error as the view of a fellow human being, but it cannot recognize it. The Buddha said: 'If you reject the insight of my teaching, you must follow your insight.' That is the legitimate, indeed necessary, tolerance of the *quest for* truth. For me, as a scientist, that is spoken from the heart. But that does not mean that science relativizes the truth that is sought. Only when you have recognized the insight of my teaching as true should you follow my teaching. And I, as a scientist, as a matter of course allow you to refute me if you can.

Since people with religious questions seek truth, they will not ultimately go along with the tolerance which is initially accepted in the global ethic. Religion is incomplete. The true religious task will also prove to lie both in a global ethic and beyond a mere global ethic. All theologies will be fundamentally changed.

I shall allow myself a last example, taking up the quotation from the Dalai Lama given above. On the eightieth birthday of the Jesuit father and Zen master Hugo Enomiya-Lassalle, a Festschrift appeared under the title *Munen-Muso*, which is the Zen name for the supreme stage of meditation, meditation with no object. Of course both Buddhists and Christians wrote in this Festschrift. What encounters us at this highest level of experience? The vocabularies used were different. The Christians said, 'Here you are encountered by the wholly Other, God.' The Buddhists said, 'Here you are encountered by your own true self.' But where the experience was described in the texts only in hints, the reader could hardly detect any difference. And the traditional Christian formula *Unio Mystica* alludes to this impossibility of differentiation.

I dare not predict where the experience of catastrophes and the new human insight into thought, action and perception will lead in the coming centuries.

My Prayer

YEHUDI MENUHIN

The author is one of the most distinguished musicians of our time

To Thee Whom I do not and cannot know – within me and beyond me – and to Whom I am bound by love, fear and faith – to the One and to the Many – I address this prayer:

Guide me to my better self – help me make myself into one who is trusted by living things, creatures and plants, as well as the air, water, earth and light that sustain these, keep me as one who respects the mystery and the character of every variety of life in both its uniqueness and its mass, for all life is essential to its own survival.

Help me to preserve my capacity for wonder, ecstasy and discovery, allow me everywhere to awaken the sense of beauty, and with and for others and for myself to contribute to the sum of beauty we behold, we hear, we smell, taste or touch or are otherwise aware of through mind and spirit; help me never to lose the life-giving exercise of protecting all that breathes and thirsts and hungers; all that suffers.

Help me find a balance between the longer rewards and the shorter pleasures, while remaining in tune with relative values, while patiently according the passage of time its rich harvest of loyalties, experience, achievement, support and inspiration.

Help me be a good trustee for the body You gave me. No life is to do with as I will, not even my 'own', for it is like an object entrusted into 'my' temporary keeping to bequeath back into the earthly cycle in the best possible condition for other life to continue.

Therefore, Thy will be done.

May those who survive me not mourn but continue to be as helpful, kind and wise to others as they were to me. Although I would love to enjoy some years yet the fruits of my lucky and rich life, with my precious wife, family, music, friends, literature and many projects, in this world of diverse cultures and peoples I have already received such blessing, affection and protection as would satisfy a thousand lives.

Allow me to see and to feel and to try to ponder and to understand the relationship of the unity of the trinity in all its manifestations.
– Birth, life and death
– creation, conservation and destruction
– Mother, Father and Child – and for the Child: Mother, Father and Teacher
– and for the parents and teacher: child, student and equal
– past, present and future
– body, mind, and soul or spirit
– self, family and friends
– love, indifferences and hate
– skill, craft and art
– solid, liquid and gas
– light, heat and sound
– time, space and subject
– the regional, the state and the community of states
– and many more trinities

Help me in all confrontations to see the 'trialogue' as opposed to the 'dialogue'. Help me so that I may decide wisely on such apportionment of pleasure and pain as may fall within my jurisdiction.

And finally, whilst begging Thee to protect me from anger and condemnation, my own of others and others of mine, allow me unpunished to indulge in my particular aversions:

Those who would exploit or corrupt for the sake or the abuse of power or money or self-indulgence – for want of a higher mode of satisfaction; from the petty bureaucrat to the ignorant and prejudiced; help them see and confess to You in themselves the error of their ways.

Enlighten them and me and help us to forgive each other.

Also with such enemies as I may possibly have, help me distinguish between the reconcilable and the irreconcilable, encourage me to seek by every means understanding with the one whilst rendering the other ineffective, to learn from both and not deliberately to antagonize either.

Grant me the inspiration you have provided humanity and encourage me to revere and to follow those living examples who enshrine your spirit – the spirit within and beyond each of us – the spirit of the One and the Many – the illumination of Christ, of Buddha, of Lao-Tse and of the prophets, sages, philosophers, poets, writers, painters, sculptors, all creators and artists, and all the selfless people, the saints and the mothers, the known and unknown, the exalted and the humble, men – women – children of all times and all places – whose spirit and example remain with us and in us forever.

From the World of Judaism

An Answer from Jerusalem on the Project of a Global Ethic

TEDDY KOLLEK

*The author was mayor of Jerusalem from 1965 to 1993.
He wrote this contribution in collaboration with
Professor Marcel Dubois*

The only right which a former mayor of Jerusalem may have to respond to your project on a global ethic based on religious traditions, consists of the fact that by virtue of his office he has personally observed the necessity, even the urgency of such a project.

One city – two peoples – three religions

Jerusalem is, for millions of people, first for those who live there, but for others throughout the world as well who believe in the God of Abraham, the source, the centre and the symbol of their faith. The office of mayor, however, is not bestowed upon one who is a theologian or a philosopher of ethics! The present situation in Jerusalem, just like the city's often tragic history throughout the centuries, raises questions about the possibility of co-existence between believers of different faiths.

One city. Two peoples. Three religions. This is the problem with which I was confronted during nearly thirty years. How to live together in a state of reciprocal acceptance and mutual respect, people who believe in the same God but whose social establishments and religious traditions are different. And it is not merely a question of the division between Jews, Christians, and Muslims: it also concerns rivalries and splits within each of these communities, between integrationists and progressives, fundamentalists and liberals, to say nothing of all the nationalistic, social and political meddling that further complicates the panoply of religious affiliations.

I often had to ask myself the question which is at the root of your project: why is religion, which is in essence a relationship with God or with the Supreme Being of the conscience and the universe, not a unifying factor, a basis for understanding, between people of faith? Why can't religions reveal the origin of a common ethic which permits differences between people, to be considered on the basis and in light of a spiritual consensus, rather than being the cause of often insoluble conflicts between people?

This is why I share both your concern and your hope. You address the same problem that I experienced in Jerusalem, but on a global human scale. It is by virtue of this experience that I feel entitled to offer you the following reflections.

The desire for an ethic out of the catastrophe

Unfortunately, one is compelled to subscribe to the characterization you present of the current state of the world in which we live: 'Hundreds of millions of human beings on our planet increasingly suffer from unemployment, poverty, hunger, and the destruction of their families. Hope for a lasting peace slips away from us. There are tensions between the sexes and generations. Children die, kill, and are killed. More and more countries are shaken by corruption in politics and business. It is increasingly difficult to live together peacefully in our cities because of the social, racial, and ethnic conflicts, the abuse of drugs, organized crime and even anarchy. Even neighbours often live in fear of one another. Our planet continues to be ruthlessly plundered. A collapse of the ecosystem threatens us.' I could illustrate this sombre inventory with numerous examples from my personal observation, within the recent history of the Near East.

This state of affairs is the result of a failure of humanity. Although many are tempted to define modernity by the extraordinary development of knowledge and technology in every field, one cannot be blind to the fact that people have never been so unhappy or so threatened in terms of their own humanity. We must duly recognize that 'Man' has not been faithful to his calling as 'Man' with regard to both himself and the spiritual dimension, to other members of the global community and even to the equilibrium of the universe. Whether by egotism or by ignorance, humanity has far too often flouted the rules of co-existence with others. This list of failures and catastrophes makes us feel the urgent need for an ethic upon which all people agree, no matter what the differences between them are in terms of traditions, philosophies, creeds, cultures and civilizations. Our world is in need of an ethic which calls each and every one of us back to our identity as a spiritual entity, which reminds us of the common fate we necessarily share with the rest of humanity, and which evokes our solidarity with the entire cosmos.

It is true that for many people, religion alone, in the unity of its essence and no matter what different forms it takes, is capable of countering this decadence, and reversing this sense of dark determinism.

In this respect, one can only agree with the 'four irrevocable directives' which you propose for the elaboration of a global ethic: non-violence and respect for life; solidarity and just economic order which requires from everyone moderation and modesty; mutual tolerance and respect for truth, demanding candour in relationships and loyalty in dialogue; equal rights and true partnership among people regardless of race, nationality, social status, and especially between men and women.

For, as you point out, the principles of such an ethic already exist in the wisdom and teachings of various religious traditions. It is possible to discern broad avenues of consensus which exist between religions, on the subject of fundamental values.

True, one may protest that the history of the religions of the world, stamped as it is with so many rivalries and conflicts, so much persecution and war, such terrible crimes and reprisals perpetrated in the name of an intolerant and exclusive idea of faith, seems to contradict this optimism. One cannot deny this cruel reality; but one may nevertheless imagine that if the faithful of diverse traditions have accomplished such acts of violence it is because they were in contradiction to the spirit of the teachings which their faith itself entails.

You are correct in saying that 'despite their frequent abuses and failures, the communities of faith bear a responsibility to demonstrate that hope in a global ethic is possible. Without ignoring the serious differences among the individual religions, they should not hinder us from proclaiming publicly those things which we already have in common and which we jointly affirm, each on the basis of our own moral or ethical grounds.'

How can one describe a universal ethic like this? You are right to underscore the paradox, even the apparent contradiction of such an undertaking. To do so, one must express a fundamental consensus 'without reducing the religions to an ethical minimalism' but rather 'representing the minimum of what the religions of the world have in common now in the ethical spheres'. You are also correct in emphasizing that we are not concerned here with devising a synchronized plan, as misguided as it is generous, in which individual identities would disappear. Nor are we interested in arriving at a poor compromise or a common denominator of mediocrity. On the contrary, the aim is to formulate rules which follow from a common perception of the profound calling of humanity, both with regard to ourselves and with regard to others. The idea is not to flatten or raze, but rather to promote the values according to which the great religions intersect. The paradox is that this common reflection requires that each religious tradition be faithful to itself, and that it finds at the same time within this fidelity the conditions for encountering others. That is, every believer within each tradition must recognize that which is required of him to accept others' differences.

What is required of Jews?

Thus, upon reading your proposal, I am compelled to ask myself what the project requires of the Jews. The Jewish religious tradition carries with it an ethic. And this ethic is based upon the certainty of an original calling which God has expressed. God called Abraham, and He gave the Torah to Israel as a symbol of the bond which He wanted to establish with the nation. Shema Israel. Listen, Israel. The people of the Bible are invited to listen. Their answer consists in obedience to the Word of God. The prophets of Israel and all of Jewish tradition are inescapably evoked with these words.

Elsewhere, for a Jew, Jerusalem is the privileged place where this presence was manifested. The city is, for all Jews observant and secular, the only point in time and space that God has touched, and where His presence persists. It is with this in mind, with the awareness of this evocation, that a Jew finds the source of his/her identity, just as it is within the Torah that the proper ethic can be found.

Let me add an important comment: the Jewish people have experienced solitude, jealousy and misunderstanding. The Holocaust created a deep doubt about God's promise to Irael. A unique experience of estrangement from and hostility by others, because of the people's loyalty to a specific religious identity. The entire history of the Jewish people is a spiritual adventure, from which no Jew can escape.

How can one reconcile this consciousness of uniqueness with the recognition of other religious identities? How must I communicate with all these people, believers in other religions, for whom my history is so foreign, and so often unknown, even though I view it as unique?

This question, which I ask myself as a Jew, must be asked by believers in other religions, in the very name of faithfulness to their beliefs and their traditions. How must I proceed from the uniqueness of my religious experience and the ethic which it inspires, towards an understanding of others whose experience is different and for whom the rules of acceptable behaviour seem so different from my own?

If I were to summarize the truths which shape the moral tradition of the Jewish people, I could do so by citing three propositions which I find in the Bible, this special book which contains the history and the wisdom of my people. 'Shema Israel.' Listen, Israel: 'Thou shalt love thy God with all thy heart, with all thy soul and with all thy strength; thou shalt love thy neighbour as thyself'; 'God created man in His image'. These are the affirmations which founded the ethic that rules my relationship with the world, with myself and with others. The faithful who belong to the religions of the Book find within it the foundations of their moral principles. But how is one to communicate this conviction, both religious and metaphysical, to those for whom religion does not signify a personal and unique deity, like the religions of the Far East? Our Hindu, Buddhist and Shinto sisters and brothers turn, each in their own way, toward the principle of the all, or to a fundamental nature which is beyond perception, or to an ultimate source of life within the spirit. These, our confrères, do not speak in terms of beings. They have no generative metaphysics. So, can the contents of my faith be communicated to them? Under what conditions is a common formulation possible? And ultimately, can a global ethic be formulated objectively, for religions for which the theology and metaphysics are so different?

Understanding between the religions is possible

Reflecting on this problem as a Jew, I feel that I am being invited to undertake a two-fold enterprise. On the one hand, in addition to my own identity and my own tradition, I am asked to recognize within the spiritual values, the moral principles and the behaviour of others, something corresponding to the values to which I adhere, and to which I strive to be faithful. That is to say, to discover in the attitudes of Christians, of Muslims, of Buddhists and of Shintoists the attention and the answer which God exposes to me upon giving me the Torah; to recognize the shape and the demands of the love which governs the relationships of others with their brethren; and to discern the mysterious image that they have of 'Man' as they reflect on one's conformity with one's own spiritual identity. On the other hand, I am being asked to attempt to translate and to understand within my terminology, the mentality and the culture of others.

This presumes an openness on my part towards others based on my own identity and my fidelity to myself, and through such openness, an acceptance of that which is universal. It requires that I be attentive to the spiritual identity of other people, to the way they express their humanity; and it requires that I help all people to remain faithful to their expression of humanity. Formulating a common ethic necessitates this mutual recognition and effort to communicate.

Why should it not be possible to create, from the mentalities and traditions of different religions, a principle analogous to that which Einstein defined as the law which governs relationships between physical systems? Every person should be able to translate, within the confines of his own system, the spiritual experience and moral values of others as they view them within their own system, with the understanding that each person should take care to be faithful to his/her own calling as a humane being.

In Jerusalem I witnessed great efforts at mutual understanding and co-existence between Jews, Christians and Muslims, with each soul striving to understand every other soul while remaining faithful to its own identity. I must admit that this did not happen on the scale of a mass movement. Such efforts were quite limited, and never well publicized. But they proved by their very existence that such a reality is possible. In order to understand the truth which inspired this will to co-exist, some individuals even defined the function of Jerusalem. It is in truth within the verticality of faith, in fidelity to oneself and consistency of spirit, that people of good will may meet.

All that goes up converges! What is it that countless pilgrims from all so many diverse communities come to Jerusalem for, if not the living symbol that such an encounter is indeed possible? One of the most beautiful confirmations of this is undoubtedly the recent visit of the Dalai Lama. It is in the name of his religious identity as a Tibetan monk that he came to Jerusalem to meet face to face with faithful members of the three great monotheistic religions.

This is why I view your project as an invitation which should be put into practice, on the scale of the entire planet and of all humanity. I witnessed the same phenomenon on a smaller scale, that of the city of Jerusalem. It is both an urgent and a generous undertaking, for which we all must share both the vision and the hope.

The global ethic which you describe does not only consist of promoting tolerance between the religions of the world, for this would represent merely a passive acceptance and resignation with regard to the religions of others. The problem is not to justify religious liberty, but rather to put this liberty into practice for the benefit of all. In this sort of enterprise, the variety of beliefs and religious traditions must not be a cause of rivalry or competition, but rather must constitute an invitation to set a mutual example of model comportment. On this theme, I hope that the summons with which you end the explanation of your project is well understood: 'What does each faith tradition have to say about the meaning of life and death, the enduring of suffering and the forgiveness of guilt, about selfless sacrifice and the necessity of reununciation, about compassion and joy? These will deepen and make more specific the already discernible global ethic.'

It is thus that I may summarize this project for a global ethic, for which you desire the co-operation of the religions of the world: To remind each and every human being of their human calling, and to encourage all to be faithful to the highest principles within themselves.

Judaism and a Global Ethic

JONATHAN MAGONET

The author is a biblical scholar and Principal of Leo Baeck College, London

From a study of the sources of Judaism, particularly the Talmud, it is quite possible to assert that a particular point of view on a given subject is 'authentically' Jewish. But it is also possible to prove that the opposite opinion is equally authentic. This is not altogether surprising, because it belongs to the nature of 'revealed' religions. Once the word of God has been given, canonized, and thus fixed 'for all eternity', interpretation becomes essential. Human ingenuity is almost limitless when it comes to creating seemingly closed systems of belief, and then finding ways to open them up. The very fact of having a fixed sacred text presents the challenge to every generation to understand it afresh. As the Rabbis expressed it, there are seventy faces to Torah, the teaching of God, by which they meant an infinite number of possible interpretations. The particular circumstances of a particular generation contribute to the direction those interpretations will take, and the vagaries of each new direction offer precedents for the future. Perhaps that is what actually defines a 'Scripture' – that it can never be simply ignored or taken for granted but demands of those who have received it that it be listened to, questioned, challenged, re-interpreted and then re-applied in the changed contemporary circumstances.

The ambivalence of universalism

Our own time, as reflected in the quest for a global ethic, is one where our particular world-view demands that religions dig into their myriad treasures to find those teachings that encourage mutual understanding, solidarity with and generosity of spirit towards each other. This seemingly 'self-evident' tolerance of today was not always the case. Indeed this same religious moment that calls for interfaith dialogue has also seen the renewal of the politicization of religion on an unprecedented scale, inter-religious conflict and the sanctioning of brutality, witch-hunts and genocide. The exhilarating sense that we belong to 'one world', and hence the need to find ways of mutual support and sharing, seems to be accompanied by the terrifying sense that we do indeed belong to 'one world' and therefore that which gives us our individual identity and uniqueness, our way of life, be it through our tribe, nation, people or religion, is under threat. Every expression of universal hope seems to call forth the contrary need to assert a particularistic identity, to be strengthened by a return to our 'roots', to that 'old-time religion', as remembered, imagined or re-invented for today. Thus the quest for a meeting across the religious traditions, one anchored in the sources and resources of our religious traditions, is actually one feature of a global religious revival, that is in some ways as problematic as it is full of opportunity and hope.

It is therefore very important that in seeking those formulations that express the universalism of our faith we do not sentimentalize what we find or deny that it has at the same time its own implicit dark side. For that must inevitably be the case. Religion seeks to address all aspects of human life and activity so as to 'redeem' them in some way, to offer them back to God who is their source. Yet the exploration of our complex human nature has built-in traps. In another context my colleague Lionel Blue expressed it by saying that religion seeks to make the world religious, yet all too often ends up by itself becoming worldly. The very beliefs and ideal forms of religious expression contain their own risks. We tend to assert that there is somewhere a pure religious ideal in our tradition that is perfect and can never do wrong – and that the crimes and disasters done in the name of our tradition are merely the incidental fault of human error, weakness or mischief. There may indeed be a level where this pure religion exists, but it is higher than the religious systems that we operate. Within the 'Abrahamic' faiths, our monotheism can easily become monolatry, our obedience subservience, and our enthusiasm fanaticism. So it is not only the formulations of the 'values' and 'truths' that we must investigate in the religions to which we belong, but their methods of achieving, and their commitment to, self-criticism, self-purification and repentance, *'teshuvah'*. Religious formulations are conventionally life-enhancing, tolerant and generous-spirited – how do we ensure that they are real?

The biblical foundations of a global ethic

All this is by way of introduction to examining a Jewish contribution to the quest for a global ethic. As suggested above, it is possible to find within Judaism both a tendency to seek out such general principles and an equally strong wish to view them with caution. In early rabbinic debates about the importance of the Ten Commandments, great care was taken to limit their prominence because of the fear that they would be seen as some kind of 'essence' of Judaism, whereas the Rabbis asserted that the Torah in its entirety was the word of God. Whether the 'laws' were immediately relevant or seemingly inexplicable, they carried equal weight and called for the same obedience. Who were we to judge what significance God placed upon them? (Though, at the same time, reason and pragmatism were immediately introduced when it came to establishing practice.) Nevertheless the Ten Commandments remain a central expression of a universal Jewish ethic. Moreover the tendency to seek even more basic guiding principles was always present. It can be seen in the following Talmudic passage:

Rabbi Simlai taught: Six hundred and thirteen commandments were given to Moses. Then King David reduced them
to eleven in Psalm 15, beginning: 'God, who may live in
Your tent, and dwell on Your holy mountain? One who
follows integrity, who does what is right and speaks the
truth in his heart.' The prophet Micah reduced them to three
(Micah 6.8): 'Act justly, love mercy and walk humbly with
your God.' Then came the prophet Isaiah and reduced them
to two *(Isaiah 56.1)*: 'Keep justice and act with integrity'.
The prophet Amos reduced them to one *(Amos 5.4)*: 'Seek
Me and live!'

Habakkuk also contained them in one statement *(Habakkuk 2.4)*: 'But the righteous shall live by his faith.' Rabbi
Akiba taught: 'The great principle of the Torah is expressed
in the commandment: "Love your neighbour as you love
yourself: I am the Eternal"' *(Leviticus 19.18)*. But Ben Azai
taught a greater principle: 'This is the book of the generations of man. When God created man, He made him in the
likeness of God.' *(Genesis 5.1)* *(Makkot 23b–24a; Genesis
Rabbah, Bereshit 24.7; Sifra 89b)*.

This last debate between Akiba and Ben Azai is recorded more
than once and reflects a central religious issue. What is the
difference between the two verses? The Leviticus verse finds our
obligation to our fellow human beings in their 'likeness' to
ourselves, though the phrase is difficult to understand. However, it must be noted that our 'neighbour' in its context in
Leviticus is somewhat narrowly defined as a fellow Israelite.
(Nevertheless a broader obligation is also present in the same
chapter, verse 34, where a complementary verse demands that
we love 'the stranger', the 'resident alien', the *ger*, 'as
ourselves'.) In contrast the Genesis quotation puts every human
being into the category of a person made in the image of God,
and therefore not only 'like us', but equally bearing the imprint
of our Creator. As expressed in our passage, the two verses
together define the essential oneness of humanity and our
obligation to mutual support, fellow-feeling and responsibility.

To Akiba is ascribed another attempt to sum up the 'whole of the Torah' in a single teaching (Avot d'Rabbi Natan XXVI 27a). It is the same formulation of the 'Golden Rule' earlier attributed to Hillel. Interestingly, the context of Hillel's answer is the request of a pagan to discover the 'essence' of Judaism. The story is worth repeating:

> A pagan came to Shammai (whose academy rivalled that of Hillel) and said to him: 'Accept me as a proselyte on the condition that you teach me the whole of the Torah while I stand on one foot!' Shammai drove him away with the measuring rod he held in his hand.
>
> Then he went to Hillel (renowned for his patience!) who received him as a proselyte and taught him: 'What is hateful to you do not do to your fellow; that is the whole of the Torah, all the rest is commentary. Go and learn' (Shabbat 31a).

All the above reflect a broad universalism within Jewish teaching that can ultimately be traced back to the opening chapters of Genesis. Beyond this recognition of the oneness of humanity the Rabbis asserted that certain key responsibilities are incumbent on all people. This they expressed in the concept of the Seven Noachide Laws, universally binding moral obligations given to Noah after the flood, and hence through his sons to all of humanity. They include prohibitions on idolatry, blasphemy, bloodshed, sexual sins, theft, and eating a limb from a living animal, as well as the positive command to establish a legal system (Tosefta Avodah Zarah 8:4; Sanhedrin 56a).

In any attempt to find a core set of universal values to which all different faith communities might be expected to subscribe, these seven laws are a possible starting point and offer a Jewish contribution to the debate. Clearly problems will emerge over definitions of idolatry, particularly given the strictness of the monotheistic faiths on this issue. The demand for establishing courts of law, so as to ensure that there is justice for all, is particularly important, even though societies disagree with each other as to what exactly constitutes 'human rights'. However, one element seemingly missing in this list is anything that addresses the question of how societies are to meet across their particular boundaries – whether the 'society' in question be a national, ethnic, religious or other kind. Where is the ethical demand to create a positive relationship with others?

For the sake of peace

In fact it exists elsewhere in a rabbinic concept: *mipnei darkei shalom*, 'in the interests of peace'. This phrase appears in the Mishnah (Gittin 5.8) in a series of regulations designed to prevent unnecessary conflict within Israel. However, the last in the series discusses the parts of the produce of the harvest that are to be left for the poor – the individual stalks of grain (gleanings), the 'corner of the field', *peah* (Leviticus 19.9) and an entire sheaf if it has been overlooked in the gathering (Deuteronomy 24.19).

They do not try to prevent the poor among the Gentiles from gathering 'gleanings', the 'forgotten sheaf' and 'the corner' – in the interests of peace.

The Talmud then elaborates:

> One provides for the poor of the Gentiles as well as the poor of Israel, and visits the sick of the Gentiles as well as the sick of Israel and buries the dead of the Gentiles as well as the dead of Israel – in the interests of peace (Gittin 61a).

A variation reads:

> In a city where there are both Jews and Gentiles, the collectors of alms collect both from Jews and from Gentiles: they feed the poor of both, visit the sick of both, bury both, comfort the mourners whether Jews or Gentiles, and they

restore the lost goods of both – in the interests of peace (Jerusalem Talmud Demai 4.6).

Presumably this idea can be traced back to Jeremiah's letter to the exiles in Babylon, encouraging them to 'seek the peace of the city to which I have exiled you, for in their peace will be your peace' (Jeremiah 29.7). At its face value, Jeremiah's call can be seen purely in terms of 'enlightened self-interest'. But pragmatic motivations are of enormous importance in establishing the base line, commonsense presuppositions for any human interaction. The process of operating on such a basis has its own rewards in the mutual respect and ultimately affection that it creates. Thus the ethos of establishing norms for relationships with the 'other' on the principle of 'in the interests of peace' has enormous long-term value and importance. Indeed its apparent 'pragmatism' conceals a fundamental religious value. The process that is initiated by this Declaration already challenges each of our faith communities to explore their equivalent teachings in this very specific area. How far do the 'interests of peace' with others affect the conventional attitudes, practices or formulations within our tradition? It is no accident that the principle emerged in Israel in a situation of relative powerlessness where accommodation to a majority power made it an essential factor for survival. Where a faith community experiences itself as having some measure of power, or, paradoxically, where that sense of power is under threat, the need for such considerations may well seem less relevant or urgent. But the challenge of 'a global ethic' lies precisely in recognizing the vulnerability of all of us and the need to reassess on all levels issues of seeming power and authority.

This latter consideration brings us back to the paradox I mentioned before – that the quest for a global ethic comes precisely at the time when enormous energies are pushing people in the opposite direction, towards a ghettoization of their particular faith community, often accompanied by expressions of hostility towards others. Those who have been engaged in 'dialogue' of any sort know that it is a two-way process. In addressing 'the other' we risk losing touch with our own community. In fact it is usually easier to deal with those from the other faith who have a similar interest in dialogue than with our co-religionists. The hardest part of dialogue is often returning home and trying to convey to those who have not had our experience what it means and why it is important, and reassuring them that we have not simply betrayed them. The success of this new initiative will depend on the degree to which we are able to enter the dialogue 'back home' and the way in which we help each other to achieve this. It is precisely at this point that formulations have to be translated into a new self-awareness, and that a transformation has to take place on intellectual, emotional and spiritual levels. Yet for this to work, we who are engaged in the task of dialogue with each other must work on such transformations within ourselves. In this case the mediator is the message. It is the committed individual who has to hold and somehow resolve the paradoxes of the different ideas within our traditions, the tensions between the particular and the universal. But more than that, he or she has to face and somehow work through the deep fears of powerlessness, alienation and dissolution that are the shadow side of our 'global village'.

No Jewish contribution would be complete without a Jewish story. A man sent his son to the *yeshiva*, the Talmudic academy, to study Talmud for five years. When he returned the father met him, took him aside into his study and asked him what he had learnt. The son replied: 'I learnt that the greatest teaching is "you shall love your neighbour as yourself".' 'But you knew that before you went away!' said the father. 'You didn't need five years of study to find that out!' 'The difference,' said the son, 'is that now I know that it means: "I must love my neighbour as myself"!'

Foundations for a Global Ethic according to the Bible, the Gospels and the Qur'an

ANDRÉ CHOURAQUI

The author is a writer; he also translates and comments on the Bible and the Qur'an in Jerusalem

For the ancients, all the rules of life in society, laws, ethics and cultural practices were grounded in God, and consequently in the revelations of them received by God's prophets. In the beginning all peoples find their ideals and their laws in revelations made to their prophets by their deities or their divinized kings. Thus for the Hebrews the Torah, and for the Christians after them the Gospels, contain not only a collection of laws of divine origin but also all the wisdom and all the ethics of the universe. Moses received the laws which he imposed on the Hebrews directly from the Hebrew Elohims (I use this strange form deliberately, for reasons which will emerge in due course). Jesus fulfilled its commandments and founded the church that we know. In the seventh century, at a time when Israel and the church were undergoing a profound crisis, a new prophet, Muhammad, founded a new religion, Islam. His revealed book, the Qur'an, endorses the teachings of the Bible and the Gospels.

On the basis of the Holy Scriptures, the Hebrews had developed a vast legal system based on the Hebrew Bible. The Mishnah and the Talmud, along with the Bible, are normative sources for the organization and life of the Jews in exile. Canon law regulates the life of Christians. It contains all the legal rulings of the Catholic Church and by extension those which govern other Christian confessions. In Islam *fiq*, or the science of law, covers everything relating to the elaboration, justification and application of the law, in the name of God. Its immediate foundation is the Revelation made to Muhammad by Allah, itself founded on the Torah of Moses and the Gospel of Jesus.

Global ethic and covenant

The three religions which emerged from these revealed texts came into being at different times, in very different historical, linguistic and cultural contexts. They developed theologies which, stemming from the same texts, are nevertheless hostile to one another. However, the new dimensions of the modern world are compelling religions to emerge from their isolation. These religions are encountering one another in every sphere of human activity, including the television screen, which brings into homes quite indiscriminately, among other messages, those of the church, the mosque or the synagogue. These facts are forcing the religions to return to their sources. And the sources refer them to their common roots, the deity of Adonai YHWH Elohims, the Creator of the heavens and earth, to his transcendent unity which is manifested in the order of the covenant.

What we now call a global ethic is fully expressed in the demands of the covenant, which we find in identical form in the three testaments. In the Hebrew Bible the covenant, *berit*, is a word derived from a root which also denotes creation, *beria*. The fact of having a single Creator is the basis for the ontological unity of the whole creation, and also of humankind, born from a single couple, Adam and Eve. The theology and ethics born of the biblical revelation can be found in similar if not identical perspectives in the Hebrew Bible, the New Testament and the Qur'an. The unity of Elohims, the creation of the universe and the finality of the universal covenant are characteristics of the biblical revelation.

In the Hebrew Bible, the expression *karat berit*, 'cut a covenant', denotes an action which, around a sacrifice, consecrates the alliance of the parties involved, an individual or a people, with Adonai YHWH Elohims, between two persons, two peoples or two partners (Gen. 21.22–32; 31.44–54; II Sam. 3.13–21; I Kings 5.26; II Kings 5.3; Ezek. 16.8; Prov. 2.17; Job. 5.23; 40.28; Isa. 28.15, 18). The covenant is a rite which manifests the unity of the Creator in the diversity, not to say the contradictions, of humanity. It is the motive force of the Unity and his expression in reality. The Pentateuch, endorsed by the prophets, defines several types of covenant. Those of Adam and Noah relate to the whole of humanity under a planetary law, the heavenly sign of which is the rainbow. The covenant of Abraham is restricted to the descendants of Israel and Ishmael, 'as numerous as the stars of heaven', and its sign is circumcision. The Mosaic covenant relates to a particular people, Israel. Its law, the Torah, gives it the vocation of being the people of the covenant, and its destiny is to become the universal instrument of the covenant of the peoples.

The Bible rightly calls itself the Book of the Covenant, and the New Testament the Book of the New Covenant. The term *diatheke* is used in Greek with the threefold meaning of Torah, revelation and promise. Thus the Bible as a whole is not concerned to found an empire or a new religion, but rather to realize the covenants of all peoples, nations or religions on earth, as an expression of their ontological unity. We find the same aims of the revealed Word in the Qur'an. The revelation of Allah, made to the prophet Muhammad, arose to authenticate the Torah and the Gospels and to confirm the aims of the covenant, *al-'ahd, mithaq*, or *'aqd*.

Hebrew *berit*, New Testament *diatheke*, Qur'anic *al-'ahd, mithaq*, or *'aqd:* these terms, drawn from three testaments, three languages, three cultures, three eras, are the basis of the internal dynamic of the three religions whose cradle lies mainly in the East, in Jerusalem. This covenant, which is essential, ontological, for these three universes, allowed Israel to survive its exiles and preserve its language, the Hebrew of the Bible, and culture. It has inspired on a universal scale the vast communities of the Christian churches and the House of Islam (*Dar-al-Islam*). The Declaration of the Parliament of the World's Religions would be reinforced by the reconciliation, around the notion of covenant, of all those who have a share in the biblical heritage, Israel, the Christians and the Muslims.

The encounter of the Abrahamic religions

Their new covenant (Jer. 31.31) could realize the messianic visions of their prophets if they gathered around the perfect transcendence of the Creator, for the salvation of creation. The essential character of YHWH, the God of Moses, of Jesus and of Muhammad, is his transcendence. He is an Elohims with no name that can be pronounced, without discernible form, pure power, unique in his creative essence of being and life. Creation of the universe, YHWH Adonai is the Elohims of Elohims, the Adon of Adonims. For rather than claiming that there is only one God, the Bible states that the Elohims are one.

In Hebrew the name Elohim is a plural (hence my rendering of it), which the translations of the Bible have ignored since the Septuagint, rather than simply transcribing YHWH Elohims, translated it *Kyrios Theos*. The name YHWH situates the God of the Bible in his pure ontological transcendence at the source of creation. YHWH is also the God of the Elohims, at the root of their universal unity. In him, Being of all being, is summed up the life and unity of all conscious beings, the one who is neither high in the heavens nor deep in the earth, but 'in the heart and on the lips of all human beings'.

The present encounter of the three Abrahamic religions is compelling thinking elites to re-examine their consciences in a way which is unprecedented in the past of Judaism, Christianity and Islam. During the two millennia of their exile, the Jews had been imprisoned in the narrow limits of their ghettos. They had only one aim, to preserve their national, cultural and linguistic identity. Now that they have been saved in a miraculous way and returned to their ancestral land, the framework of traditional Jewish thought has been exploded. Having returned to the sources of their revelation and their exilic religion, Jews note that their turning in on themselves, which has preserved their identity, would be the death of them if they did not open up to the dimensions of the world in the land they have regained. And in the world, they must first become open towards Christianity and Islam in the East where they are again putting down roots.

Christians for their part are equally aware of the fact that they are a minority in two ways. The time of Catholic, Orthodox or Protestant triumphalism is over: on a planetary scale all the Christian churches taken together constitute a minority by comparison with the non-Christian religions of Asia, Africa and America. This minority is further reduced if we reflect on the rapid progress of atheism, agnosticism and materialism in Christian countries. The massive desertion from the churches is forcing the theologians of these churches to reconsider their thought, and even their dogma.

Even the Catholic Church, which is the most hierarchical church, convened a council on the prompting of John XXIII under the irresistible pressure of the facts. The decisions of Vatican II, in particular the Declaration *Nostra Aetate*, have opened up a new future to relations between Christianity and the non-Christian world. To begin with, John XXIII and Cardinal Bea had wanted to normalize relations between the Holy See and the Jews. This problem led the Catholic Church to redefine its standpoint not only towards the Jews but also towards all the other religions. This vast movement ended in a gathering of the main religions at Assisi.

The basic act of recognition between the Holy See and the State of Israel, signed in Jerusalem and Rome on 30 December 1993, was not just a treaty between two states. It normalized a situation which had been compromised, since the birth of the church, by the destruction of Hebraic Judaea and the exile of the Jews. The rebirth of the State of Israel brought the Jews back to their original homeland where the resurrection of the Hebrew language opened up a new era in the history of Jerusalem, city of origins, in its mediating vocation. The reciprocal recognition of the church and Israel will restore to Christianity its historical roots and to Judaism its fruits – both the result that they hope for.

The hope for peace through the religions

Israel is in a crisis of growth. Formed in 1948, the new-born nation is so to speak in search of its new identity, very different from the Jewish identity in the exile. Like the church, it faces the problems posed to all by the developments of the modern world. The same crisis is causing great turbulence in Muslim countries. In a few decades, since the end of the Second World War, they have passed from the colonial age to independence. Furthermore, rejecting the creation of the State of Israel on 15 May 1948, they have been engaged in a bloody conflict which in seven wars has brought the deaths of tens of thousands in both camps and has swallowed up for decades the vital forces of the two peoples and their allies.

Here, too, an era of peace was opened up by the agreements signed in Washington on 13 September 1993 between Israel and the Palestine Liberation Organization. These agreements have set in motion a peace process in the Middle East between the Arab world and the Jewish world. The handshake between Yasser Arafat, President of the PLO, and the Israeli Prime Minister Itzhak Rabin, was followed on 25 July 1994, also in Washington under the Presidency of Bill Clinton, by agreement between Israel and the Hashemite Kingdom of Jordan represented by King Hussein and Prime Minister Rabin. The frontier between these two countries, which had been closed for almost half a century, was solemnly opened on 8 August 1994.

These overtures between Israel, the Christian world and Islam are beyond doubt the beginning of an era of peace between three religions which, rooted in the same biblical culture, proclaim the same God and essentially the same ethic, of Torah, Gospel and Qur'an. The modern echo of this ethic can be found in the aspirations expressed in the 1948 Universal Declaration of Human Rights and more recently in the Declaration on a Global Ethic of the Parliament of the World's Religions, which has revived the great ideals of brotherhood, peace, union between different ethnic groups, peoples, nations, churches.

It is to be hoped that this Declaration prefigures the future of our reconciliation. It is also to be hoped that the peoples established all round the Mediterranean, Christians, Muslims or sons of Israel, will do pioneer work here. And it is to be hoped that we shall see established around Jerusalem a confederation of the three peoples which have their roots there, and the three religions which lay claim to it, reconciled within a Euro-Mediterranean Union dedicated to realizing in our day the ancient prophecy made to Abraham: 'In your seed shall all the nations of the earth bless themselves (Genesis 22.18; 26.4; 12.3).

The World Seeks Moral and Spiritual Leadership

SIR SIGMUND STERNBERG

The author is Chairman of the Executive Committee of the International Council of Christians and Jews in London

'Joint trustees' is how Lord Coggan, a former Archbishop of Canterbury, described the task of the Council of Christians and Jews at a special service at St Paul's Cathedral, London to mark the fiftieth anniversary of the Council.

'Our world,' he said, 'needs to hear of a God who is at once a God of love and a God of justice. A God who cares for his creation and for every human being made in his image. A God who has committed to his creatures the care of his world and made them trustees of the earth and all that is in it. A God who has put within his children the vision of his kingly reign and bidden them share in its coming. That is our greatest treasure.'

Bringing together people of faith

The hope has always been that CCJ would witness to the moral values shared by Jews and Christians. The same hope inspires the International Council of Christians and Jews. The ICCJ is the umbrella organization of twenty-six national Jewish-Christian dialogue organizations world-wide which deals with relations between Christians and Jews, the oldest prejudice and enmity burdening inter-religious relations. Its activities, whilst concentrating on Jewish-Christian relations, serve as a model for wider interfaith relations and interfaith bodies, such as the World Congress of Faiths and the World Conference on Religion and Peace.

Whilst all these organizations have sought to unite people of faith to address the moral issues facing humankind and to work together for peace and justice, much of their work has consisted in clearing the ground to make this possible. They have had to hack down the giant weeds of prejudice and misinformation that have cut people off from each other. They have done a great educational work in helping people to learn about each other's religions and to meet and get to know each other. The transformation in Jewish-Christian relations since the war is evidence of this.

It is not, however, enough. The great achievement of the Chicago Parliament of the World's Religions in 1993 was to focus attention on what the religions have to say together to a world in a crisis – to a world looking for moral and spiritual leadership. That the members of the Assembly of Spiritual and Religious Leaders were able to agree on a Declaration Toward a Global Ethic was largely due to the thorough preparatory work of Professor Hans Küng and those who have worked with him.

It is important that the document is widely discussed and especially that it is used in the moral education of the young.

Towards a 'World Council of Faiths'

The continuing question is how the insights of the great religions can be brought to bear on the political and economic issues of the day. This concern is especially relevant as the United Nations prepares to celebrate its fiftieth anniversary.

In Chicago, Lord Coggan spoke about 'the need for a World Council of Faiths through which religious leaders could meet together to address the key issues of the day and which would help to make their voice clearly heard. No immediate steps have been taken to create such a body, but I am glad that various related initiatives are being taken. It is important that all concerned for moral values in our world work together.'

'That is why,' he continued, 'I believe the creation of the International Interfaith Centre at Oxford is so important.' This Centre is intended to be:

- an education centre to promote research into ways of developing inter-religious understanding and to relate the academic study of religions to interfaith activity;
- a co-ordinating centre to facilitate co-operation between all those actively engaged in interfaith work;
- a support centre to strengthen personal contact between those who are involved in interfaith work;
- a spiritual centre to provide opportunities for deep understanding of prayer, worship and meditation in the world's religions.

In his introduction to the global ethic, Hans Küng, who has done so much in this field, speaks of the hope that this document may set off a process which changes the behaviour of men and women in the religions in the direction of understanding, respect and co-operation. I believe that the Declaration is already doing this, but that to achieve the Declaration's full potential, all interfaith bodies need to make it central to their programmes. There is an enormous reservoir of good will and creative energy in our faith communities, which, if we harness it, can set our world free from its present agony.

Towards an Ethic which Honours Humankind and the Creator

ELIE WIESEL

The author is a writer and has been awarded the Nobel Peace Prize

If in the end morality could be defined by criteria of nationality and religion, the same cannot be said of ethics, which can only be conceived of in global terms.

One could almost say that by its very nature and in its objectives, ethics is called on to transcend all that separates beings. In other words, there is no such thing as a national or ethnic, political or spiritual ethic – or rather, such a thing should not exist. An ethic centred on itself, obsessed with itself, is not an ethic.

An ethic implies my relations with others or the Other. Whatever his or her faith may be, wherever he or she comes from, the other has the right to his or her share of happiness and truth, just as I have a right to mine. To deny the other this right would be to humiliate him or her. Now the opposite of all ethics is not sin in the religious sense, but humiliation in the human sense.

That is why, at the end of this century and this millennium, it is incumbent on all those who still believe in universal humanity, i.e. the universality of human beings, to proclaim the sovereignty of ethics and to declare it humane and humanizing only if its character is global.

In other words, even if the religion of the Jew is different from the religion of the Muslim, the Christian or the Buddhist, what they have in common is the possibility and the need to declare themselves united in one and the same ethic – the ethic which honours humanity and thus also honours the Creator.

Signs of Hope

A letter about the global ethic

*The author was a professor at the Sorbonne and is
Chief Rabbi of France*

Dear Professor,

Many thanks for your letter and for the French translation of
the Declaration on a Global Ethic.

I am very aware of the honour that you have sought to do me
and would like to assure you that I totally support the
Declaration which you have formulated in such a remarkable
way. I associate myself with it fully and unreservedly.

You have managed to avoid all religious syncretism and to
show absolute respect, as you always do, for the specific
features of each of the religions of the Book, and beyond that
of all the spiritual and ethical sensibilities of humankind.

However, if you will allow it, I would like to add a second
part to your Declaration, one that brings out the prime
importance of education and teaching, in particular the
teaching of morality which, in our secularized societies, is at
best regarded as a poor relation, both in terms of the
importance accorded to this discipline, which remains fundamental, and the number of hours of teaching alloted to it.

Furthermore, and above all, I think that we must give pride
of place to hope. Certainly the world as you have described it
runs the risk of being 'in agony' in a destruction worse than
that of the Flood or of Sodom and Gomorrah. But some signs

are particularly encouraging, and compensate for the disench-
antment which perhaps comes through in the first pages of
your Declaration:
– The collapse of Communism, the first shoots of democracy
in Eastern Europe, which give us reason to hope that the reign
of the lie is over and the reign of democracy is appearing on the
horizon.
– The extreme modesty of scientists who, in contrast to their
predecessors at the end of the nineteenth century, now
understand that science will not resolve all problems and will
not conquer death. The anguished appeal which they are
making to the representatives of religion and specialists in
ethics shows that science has ceased to be an idolatry and is
progressively putting itself at the service of the virtuous and
the good.
– The establishment of a sincere peace in the Middle East, a
peace of the heart, which we have hoped for so passionately
and which seemed in the sphere of the utopian or the
impossible. I had the infinite privilege of being present in
Jerusalem, the city of peace, at the time of the signing of the
peace treaty between Israel and Jordan: fifteen years ago now a
peace treaty was signed with Egypt, and one has recently been
signed with the Palestinians. Beyond any question these are
forerunners of those which will soon be signed with Syria and
Lebanon, and, one day, with Iraq and then with Iran.
– Finally, the revival of religious feeling which we are now
witnessing. This runs the risk of bringing considerable danger,
in the form of integralism, fundamentalism, intolerance and
regression at a moral and an intellectual level, and so on. But it
also brings a great hope, that of a return to the true religious
values that the Book has affirmed to the world: love of the
stranger; tolerance and respect of the other; the feeling that we
are all equal because we are all created in the image of God;
and above all the freedom that the Transcendent has granted
us, making us equal partners in dialogue, face to face. This
freedom entails a sense of our responsibility and openness to a
radiant, limitless hope.

From the World of Christianity

The Human Race as a Community of Destiny

FRANZ KÖNIG

The author was Archbishop of Vienna from 1956 to 1985 and is a cardinal of the Roman Catholic Church

The dropping of the first atom bombs on the Japanese cities of Hiroshima and Nagasaki on 6 and 9 August 1945 was a signal for all humankind. The possibility of the world-wide destruction of great cities, fertile land, countless innocent people, made the mere existence of nuclear weapons a question-mark against the very future of the world. This led Albert Einstein, who was awarded the Nobel Prize for Physics, to comment that the power of the atom which had been unleashed had changed everything, but not our thought. However, if humanity was to survive, that too had to change.

Putting a global ethic in the religious heritage of humankind

Similarly, some years ago, in his *Global Responsibility*, translated into many languages, Professor Küng pointed out that the world in which we live, the new 'world society', does not need a single unified religion or a single, unified ideology but 'does need some norms, values, ideals and goals to bring it together and to be binding on it'. For, he added critically, 'humankind can less and less afford religions stirring up wars on this earth instead of making peace . . . practising superiority instead of engaging in dialogue' (xvi).

He summed up his concern like this: 'It is probable that consciousness of our global responsibility for the future of humankind has never been so great as it is now. Abstinence in matters of ethics is no longer possible. It has become abundantly clear why we need a global ethic. For there can be no survival without a world ethic' (69). Here, too, we can see as it were an answer to Einstein's assertion: our thought must change if we want to survive.

My concern is to put such a 'project' of a global ethic more strongly within the religious heritage of humankind. A 'global ethic' from a European perspective, associated with European criticism of religion and the history of religion, can run the risk of becoming isolated. On the other hand, comparative religion and the history of religions with their vast geographical extent and historical dimensions have given us an amazing view of what Mircea Eliade has called the 'religious experience of all humankind'. Here Christianity, too, is in process of being given a new status. Criticism of religion no longer primarily has Christianity in view, as used to be the case. A 'World Conference of the Religions for Peace' can now already count on the co-operation of Catholic Christians in ecumenical collaboration.

Nowadays it is said that the science of religion is a science of religious people (thus Holsten). Religion is always concerned with human beings and the great variety of their culture. For a long time there was little reflection on the fact that religion is not only a science but above all is rooted in human beings and can only be understood through human beings in their history. Traces left behind in history must be connected with those from whom they come, i.e. human beings. Traces and indications of the religious life of extinct peoples and cultures can only be researched to some degree by inferences and by their human points of reference. So it must be emphasized once again that the science of religion is a science of the religious person.

Here we also need to understand the many forms of abuse, the misinterpretations of religion and the religious, which can be found through all our errant human ways, to the point of strife and war in the name of faith or heresy.

That makes things more difficult, not easier. And it tells us that human beings – despite everything – in the present and the past, in all cultures and epochs of history, know themselves to be dependent on divine powers or a supreme being. They also experience their destiny in different ways, in the direction of 'another world'. And they interpret their 'mystery' in terms of that.

The questions 'Where do I come from?', 'Where am I going?' and 'What is the meaning of my life?' touch on the nature and the whole historical existence of human beings. They seek an answer to the unsolved riddle of human existence from the different religions; there are questions which have always deeply moved the human heart: 'What is the ultimate mystery, beyond human explanation, which embraces our entire existence, from which we take our origin and towards which we tend?' (Second Vatican Council, *Nostra Aetate*, no. 1).

Taken in isolation, an abstract theoretical knowledge of similar forms of expression, or forms of expression which remain the same, expressions that are to be found in many religions, does not lead to a greater knowledge of what religion is. If there is no personal experience of a religious life, the great wealth of knowledge we have about the history of religions is often dead knowledge. But if a personal religion is combined with the study of the history of religion, it can bring great enrichment. For it not only communicates a deeper knowledge of human beings in all times and cultures, but also leads us to wonder at the wealth of images and forms in the religions of past times which have found or still find expression in the history of individuals, peoples and cultures.

So in my view it is the task of ecumenical and inter-religious dialogue, exercising a great deal of patience, to make the human basis of the 'religion' better known. This will serve towards mutual understanding on the one hand and towards the demolition of existing tensions, conflicts and prejudices on the other. It calls for respect for one's partner and clarity about one's own position.

Peace – a task for the religions

Today, we are all becoming more aware how as a result of developments in communication, science and transport the human race has a common destiny. This awareness can be deepened and extended by ecumenical or inter-religious dialogue. This already brings out the fact that peace is not just a matter of discussions and conferences, but is not least also a matter of reforming dispositions and hearts, as can be done by religion.

An attempt of this kind took place in Assisi in October 1986. The supreme head of the Catholic Church, Pope John Paul II, had personally invited the great religions of the world to meet and to pray for world peace. On that occasion the Pope emphatically pointed out that in our time there was a new, common task for religions, to dedicate themselves to peace, which was threatened in the world, and to make this common interest known through prayer. We must not lose sight of the fact that prayer is the foundation of all religion. It builds the personal bridge from the world of the transitory to that other world towards which the longing of seeking and questioning men and women is directed.

In a European perspective, dialogue between the monotheistic religions has priority. There are three different ways of faith which have as their common ground belief in the one God, the one creator of heaven and earth. This is not a chance historical similarity, but one and the same basic notion of one living God who exists in himself and has communicated himself to human beings. From the perspective of religious studies generally, it is a phenomenon of a special kind that in the incredible wealth of the religious history of humankind so far investigated, no one else, no tribe and no people, has faith in the one, sole God in the way that the three monotheistic religions do. Everywhere we find a dualistic or polytheistic framework, a framework of the universal history of religion. Amarna in Egypt, which is often cited, was a brief political era with an Egyptian polytheistic background and cannot be regarded as a preliminary stage of monotheism. Something similar is true of the Zoroastrian deity Ahura Mazda. As portrayed in the Gathas, despite the eschatological perspective he remains rooted in a dualistic picture of the world.

The 'project' of a 'global ethic' as presented by Professor Küng with striking arguments therefore raises not least the question how the binding values and aims of a global society in the making – which can be recognized increasingly clearly in the global network of the media – are to relate to religion as an important concomitant factor – but only a concomitant factor. Or would such a project not be better rooted directly in the whole religious heritage of humankind? In this way a global ethic would be not only accompanied by religion, but directly supported by it.

Global Order and Global Ethic

KONRAD RAISER

The author is General Secretary of the World Council of Churches in Geneva

'Our world is experiencing a *fundamental crisis*: a crisis in global economy, global ecology, and global politics.' So begins the Declaration on a Global Ethic which was signed in September 1993 by those who took part in the Parliament of the World's Religions in Chicago.

No human rights without a basic moral consensus

The present crisis is the consequence of the globalization of almost all spheres of life which has taken place in the last two generations. However, the *de facto* globalization, which has come about above all as a result of economic interdependence, is not matched by any viable and recognized world order. International law and the international organizations are proving too weak to stem the destructive effects of rapid globalization and keep them under control. The end of the Cold War and the collapse of the bipolar system of stabilization through two great powers has brought the simmering crisis to boiling point.

How can the new world order which is so urgently necessary come about? The question itself is not new. For more than three hundred years, i.e. since the rise of the system of sovereign nation states at the end of the Thirty Years' War, efforts have been made to create a legal framework for relations between states. The two World Wars in our century helped to advance these efforts decisively. They led to the various conventions of humanitarian international law like the Geneva Convention; the basic agreements on working conditions; and above all the institutions of the League of Nations and the United Nations. In its preamble, the United Nations Charter indicates that it is no longer just concerned with ordering relationships between states. Individuals themselves, 'we, the peoples of the United Nations', are the subject of this order, which is founded on belief in the basic values of humanity, in the dignity and value of the human person, and in the equal rights of men and women and of all nations, great or small. The order is to preserve future generations from the scourge of war and to advance justice and social progress in greater freedom. The Universal Declaration on Human Rights of December 1948 formulates the common view of the rights and freedoms of all human beings as the common ideal to be attained by all peoples and nations.

Important though these elements of a world order are, they have not been able to prevent the global crisis. The flagrant violation of human rights in all parts of the world shows that the present international order is more a community of interests of the powerful, and is not primarily orientated on protecting the living conditions of ordinary people. Human rights still remain an ideal without the character of a binding obligation, and their universality is increasingly put in question.

The Declaration on a Global Ethic says, 'No new global order without a new global ethic.' Indeed – we know from the experience of developments within society that legislation without a basic moral consensus, regardless of its foundation, can easily become an instrument for the sheer exercise of power and therefore loses its legitimacy. The Universal Declaration on Human Rights was presumably understood by its authors as an expression of such a basic moral consensus. It was an expression of the basic moral values of Western bourgeois culture which in the course of the Enlightenment and secularization had become detached from the authoritative precepts of a morality grounded in the church and religion. The progressive individualization of living conditions and the overwhelming power of instrumental, utilitarian thinking has meanwhile come to undermine this moral consensus, too.

The same processes, which as a result have led to the present global crisis, are also the cause of the dissolution of the fabric of individual and social morality. Illuminating though the call is for a global ethic as a moral foundation of a new global order, it threatens to run into the sand in the face of the global crisis in all human societies which is becoming visible in the course of globalization.

A new moral culture

From the start, the ecumenical movement which has developed among Christian churches since the beginning of this century aimed not only to overcome the historical divisions between the Christian churches but also to build an international order which was to preserve peace between the nations and bring about justice, freedom and respect for human dignity. The ecumenical discussions of the 1920s and 1930s on the construction of international law and the ecumenical contributions to the formulation of the Charter of the United Nations and the Universal Declaration on Human Rights were based on the conviction that an international legal order had to be rooted in an international ethos, a common basis of moral principles.

For a long time it was presupposed in these discussions that Christianity as a religion with a universal scope and not limited by rational or cultural barriers was the only force which could hold the world together with its moral principles. At the same time, it was expected that Christian culture with its moral foundations would establish itself all over the world as traditional forms of life were displaced.

A process of profound rethinking has taken place over the

last thirty years. The churches in an ecumenical movement which is now really world-wide have become aware of their status as a minority in a pluralistic religious world. Moreover, many churches exist as tiny minorities in societies the moral basis of which is determined by other cultural and religious traditions. In this situation there must be a new critical reflection on the universal claim of a Christian ethic.

However, the originally positive view of an international order on the basis of a Christian ethic was shattered from another side. In the course of decolonialization and the wars of liberation and independence, the global order which had been handed down was increasingly strongly felt to be a decisive hindrance to the realization of justice and peace. Development, it was now said, means change and thus disorder. In view of the signs of a global crisis affecting not only the social order but also the very foundations of morality, ecumenical concerns have meanwhile increasingly been directed towards the reconstruction and safeguarding of the criteria and values which are decisive for preserving the life of human beings and nature. Hence the call for a 'new global system' which is orientated on the demands of justice, peace and the preservation of creation, which respects the cultural and spiritual multiplicity of human societies and takes account of the realities of life. Here it is clear that the issue is not just one of basic values but the development of a new form of life, a 'culture' of non-violence and reverence for life, a culture of dialogue and solidarity.

The attempts to formulate basic convictions and criteria on which such a new moral culture could be orientated go back to biblical Christian traditions. Thus they follow not so much the methods of ethical discourse, but rather a way which is indicated in the biblical tradition itself, of the presentation of collective symbols and stories in which knowledge of the conditions of successful life have been expressed. Here the concern is not so much to inculcate moral norms as an expression of the will of God as to indicate a way and the limits of possible deviations from it. This is taking place in the awareness that Christians everywhere live alongside people who have been shaped by other cultural and religious traditions and derive their moral orientation from them. The experience of inter-religious dialogue in mixed communities shows that a mutual recognition is possible which preserves the integrity of each tradition and recognizes the conditions for successful life.

What is the status and scope of a global ethic?

The Declaration on a Global Ethic goes one stage further. It seeks to root the vision of the peaceful co-existence of peoples in justice and freedom through an order safeguarded by law, which is expressed in the Universal Declaration on Human Rights, in a 'fundamental consensus on binding values, irrevocable standards, and personal attitudes'. It is confident that the different religious and ethical traditions of humankind contain sufficient elements of an ethic 'which is convincing and practical for all women and men of good will, religious and non-religious'. To some degree the Declaration attempts to make mutual recognition visible in the conditions of successful life and to maintain its central insights.

This leads to a simple and convincing basic structure. Starting from the basic conviction, 'Every human being must be treated humanely', which has been expressed in the Golden Rule known in almost all religions and ethical traditions, the Declaration identifies four 'irrevocable directives':

— You shall not kill! Or in positive terms: Have respect for life!
— You shall not steal! Or in positive terms: Deal honestly and fairly!
— You shall not lie! Or in positive terms: Speak and act truthfully!
— You shall not commit sexual immorality! Or in positive terms: Respect and love one another!

These directives aim at a culture of non-violence, solidarity, tolerance and equal rights.

In the background of this structure we can clearly recognize a recollection of the biblical traditions, especially the 'second table' of the Decalogue. But it also seeks to contribute towards the renewal of the spiritual and moral forces of the other religious traditions. The Declaration wishes 'to recall irrevocable, unconditional ethical norms. These should not be bonds and chains, but helps and supports for people to find and realize once again in their lives directions, orientations, and meaning.' The ultimate aim of the Declaration is to encourage that change of awareness without which the global crisis cannot be overcome and our world cannot be changed for the better.

The close relationship between the Declaration and the ecumenical quest mentioned earlier is unmistakable. In both instances the concern is the reconstruction of a culture which enhances life by recalling directives which have become concealed and relating them to the present day. The decisive difference is that the Declaration makes the claim to formulate elements of a global ethic which is clear to all men and women of good will, one that they can live out and is therefore also binding. The insight, veiled by experience, that no society can survive without a basic ethical consensus becomes the postulate: No new global order without a global ethic and its expression in the formulation of irrevocable unconditional ethical norms.

But is this conclusion convincing? Does what applies to each closed society apply in the same way to the global society? What is the status and scope of the 'global ethic' formulated here? Is it really meant to be normative, or rather 'regulative', in the sense of furthering mutual recognition and a change of awareness, i.e. initiating a process of common searching and understanding?

Any ethic that can be lived out is embedded in cultural and religious traditions. Moral awareness is formed through symbols, stories and rituals, which are handed down from one generation to the next. The root of any morality that can be lived out is a concrete community of people, their history, their traditions, their interpretation of the world. Ethics are like language: we can learn the rules for translation from one language to another, but the rules themselves do not produce a global language.

The Declaration on a Global Ethic formulates more the rules which can help in the process of mutual knowledge in the awareness of successful life. They can help to revive concealed knowledge and thus be a stimulus towards a change of awareness. However, the validity and binding nature of the directives can be grounded only in the different concrete contexts of traditions. This remains the limitation of any 'global ethic'.

Good pt.

Reconciliation between the Nations and the Peace of the World

PATRIARCH BARTHOLOMEW I

The author is Ecumenical Patriarch of Constantinople and has the primacy of honour within the Orthodox churches

The following text was originally given as a speech to the plenary assembly of the European Parliament in Strasbourg in 1994. It is not a direct commentary on the Declaration of the Parliament of the World's Religions, but with it I would want to draw attention to that declaration, and its impressive formulations and statements which are fundamental and therefore of universal validity.

Against the absolutizing of nationalism and racism

The unification of Europe is a task which is familiar to us. We minister to a tradition of seventeen centuries of caring and struggling for the salvation and unity of European civilization. However, the elder Patriarchate of New Rome –Constantinople, together with the other European axis, Old Rome, have not been able to make this unity visible. We are most deeply grieved by this fact. We continue, however, to pursue in common our initial witness that political unity separated from civilization, that is, without the fundamental meaning of human relationships, cannot lead to the achievement of a united Europe. The unity pursued by the peoples of Europe can only be realized as unity in the sharing of a common meaning of life, as a common goal of our human relationships.

It is surprising that the real and most deeply democratic organization of the Orthodox Christian Church with its rather large degree of administrative autonomy and local independence of its bishops, patriarchates and autocephalous churches, all simultaneously enjoying the eucharistic unity in faith, is one kind of model which the European Union under the name of the principle recently legislated as the most advantageous method for defining its powers.

In spite of the drastic world changes throughout the history of Europe, Old and New Rome continue to remain axes of reference for the unity of European civilization. We are speaking here about the fundamental meaning of unity, not an ideological alienation of this understanding into religious political doctrines which often leads to the absolutizing of nationalistic and racial particularities.

It is our belief that European unification will not be possible if such absolutes dominate. We are aware that at this very moment many of you have put before us and the Orthodox Catholic Church, which we serve in her senior-ranking diocese, the tragic reality of a horrendous war of our times in which Orthodox populations of Europe have become embroiled, where there is fighting among neighbouring Christians and people of other faiths.

The Ecumenical Patriarchate and the Orthodox Church in general respect the ethnic traditions and sensitivities of peoples. However, we most categorically condemn every kind of fanaticism, transgression and use of violence, regardless of where they come from. Our persistence in the need for free and peaceful communication among people, mutual respect and peaceful co-existence among nations remains unmoved, as we also underscored in the recent 'Bosphorus Declaration' during the conference on 'Peace and Tolerance' which was convened at our initiative.

You are the prime contributors to European unification. It is your obligation as political leaders, especially since you are the ones exercising legal authority, to see to the protection of the weak and every kind of minority, the safeguarding of freedom of thought and speech, as well as the movement and residence of persons where their natural, spiritual and social needs require. In general, it is your obligation to create those kinds of conditions which would allow for the promotion of co-operation and unity among peoples and nations. In conjunction with this is your obligation to lessen or, even more, to remove, the inequality of development which is evident between the wealthy 'developed' world and that which is undeveloped. Such inequality endangers the future of humanity.

History is moved by the 'power of weakness'

United Europe must not only offer a plan of unified economic development nor simply a programme of collective defence. With things as they are, the vision demands a unified social strategy of peaceful and constructive co-operation for the peoples of Europe. It is a question of civilization. It is a question of understanding inter-personal relationships, accepting one another's national traditions.

The Ecumenical Patriarchate of New Rome-Constantinople does not lay claim to political strength, economic power or ideological claims. This is not our mission. Permit us to note, however, that experience over the centuries paradoxically confirms that power, which continues to stimulate history, is *made perfect in weakness* (II Corinthians 12.9). We submit to you the experience of our recent efforts. Whenever we attempted to further the ecumenical unity of the Christian churches, the fruits we were worthy to receive were the product of our weakness and not of our strength. The Ecumenical Patriarchate in 1920, upon its own initiative and through an encyclical addressed to the entire world, sought to convene the churches in a kind of league modelled on the 'League of Nations', the forerunner of today's United Nations.

Through this initiative, and with the co-operation of the Protestant confessions, the World Council of Churches was founded. Here, in spite of the existing weaknesses, a certain mutual interdwelling of traditions, inter-church aid and the building of reciprocating respect is generated on the level of a cultivation of consciences.

A similar experience is derived from an equally important initiative of the Ecumenical Patriarchate to inaugurate, along with the other sister Orthodox Churches, bi-lateral theological dialogues with the ancient Oriental Churches, the Roman Catholic, the Old Catholic, the Anglican, the Lutheran and the Reformed Churches. There was a historical meeting of our predecessor, Patriarch Athenagoras, with Pope Paul VI, both of blessed memory, in Jerusalem 1964. It was the first such meeting of the primates of Old and New Rome since the Great Schism of 1054. The anathemas between these two churches were lifted in 1965 and visits exchanged between Pope John Paul II and our immediate predecessor, the late Ecumenical Patriarch Dimitrios.

We ourselves continue the effort. Recently we extended it by attempting an inter-religious rapprochement. We convened an international inter-religious conference under the aegis of the Ecumenical Patriarchate on the theme of 'Peace and Tolerance'. We are fully aware that the cultivation of a peaceful climate for co-existence and creative co-operation – both among religions and churches as well as among national states, races and traditions – demands radical change. Dialogue, international conferences, communication among leaders responsible for drafting legislation, growing closer through goodwill, and abandoning the notion of irreconcilable differences are positive, useful steps; but they are not enough. The problems of the contemporary world and the problems confronting Europe in particular demand fundamental re-evaluations of our cultural choices; in other words, the presuppositions for our cultural model.

Approaching basic problems: unemployment and the destruction of the environment

Two emphatic paradigms bear witness to this need. The first is the tragedy of *unemployment* which plagues Europe today. It is obvious that neither moral counsel nor fragmented measures of socio-economic policies are enough to confront rising unemployment. The problem of unemployment compels us to re-examine the self-evident priorities in our society, such as the absolute priority of so-called 'development', which is measured only in economic terms. We are trapped in the tyrannical need continually to increase productivity and, as a consequence, continually to create newer, and greater quantities of, consumer goods. Placing these two necessities on an equal footing imposes the constant need for greater perfection of the means of productivity while continually restricting the power of production, that is the human potential; concurrently, consumer needs of this very same human potential must constantly increase and expand. Thus, the economy becomes independent of the needs of society, functions without human intervention, and develops into industrial method which tries to equate abstract proportions.

Perhaps, because of the acute problem of unemployment, it is time, instead of concerning ourselves with self-centred demands for our individual rights, to make personal productivity within the realm of human relationships a priority. Civil management of public affairs must answer the question: who will inspire the European of today to give priority to the interpersonal relationships, and how will this be done? What will be the political mandate that will convince humankind willingly and joyfully to sacrifice its impetuous need for consumption and its limitless demands for unquenchable productivity in order to rediscover the communion of life within the community of persons?

Politics plays a role in the radical changes in understanding human life, but in people's consciences they are consolidated only by the persuasion of experiences as conveyed through the religious traditions. If the findings of the classic and renowned studies of Max Weber, Werner Sombart and R. H. Tawney hold true, then at the base of the contemporary European understanding of work and economics one can find a concrete receptiveness to Christian theology. If this holds true, a new concept of understanding work and economy will unavoidably pass through theological revision. The circumvention of theology by various ideologies has not convincingly brought about any realistic solutions. Behind the modern impasse of European life hides a theological position.

We believe that similar conclusions can be derived from the second issue equally critical and distressing in our times – the problem of *ecology*. All of us are aware of the nightmarish proportions of this problem as it increases day by day.

We are convinced that the ecological problem of our times demands a radical re-evaluation of our understanding of how we see the entire world; it demands another interpretation of matter and the world; another perception of the attitude of humankind towards nature; and another understanding of how we acquire and make use of our material goods. Within the measure of our spiritual capacity, the Orthodox Church and theology endeavours to contribute to the necessary dialogue concerning this problem. Thus, upon the initiative of the Ecumenical Patriarchate, we, the Orthodox, have established 1 September of each year as a day of meditation and prayer in confronting the continuing ecological destruction of our planet. Having convened an international conference in Crete, we have further inaugurated a systematic theological study on this problem. However, our efforts will be meaningless if they remain fragmented. Therefore we hasten to declare that we are prepared to place our modest efforts at the disposal of the European Parliament for any future study and concern of a pan-European response to the ecological problem. We declare the same readiness in reference to the aforementioned problem of unemployment plaguing Europe.

Your gracious invitation has permitted us to share this

limited but valuable time to communicate personally with you. We feel the overwhelming burden of our responsibility. We have endeavoured to review the history and the experience of an institution which for seventeen centuries has continued to function as an axis for the unity of European civilization. We aspire to continue the tradition of the Ecumenical Patriarchate of New Rome-Constantinople and to continue to preach the word of God, as did the Patriarchs of Constantinople John Chrysostom, Gregory the Theologian, Photius the Great and a myriad of giants, not only in the realm of ecclesiastical history, but also in European history.

Historical conditions have drastically changed the world scene. Please accept our presence here as a simple reminder that we exist. And we continue to minister and to bear witness to the common struggle in caring for the contribution of understanding and hope world-wide. The metropolitan sees of the Ecumenical Patriarchate in all the European countries, the hundreds of parishes of Orthodox faithful in Central and Western Europe, immigrant and local populations, are our flock and people of your political constituencies. From outside the boundaries of the twelve-nation European Union, a great number of other multi-populated nations belonging to the Orthodox ecclesiastical tradition also follow on the European journey. Permit us to express the hope that these peoples will be called soon to participate in the life and institutions of a united Europe.

Through its faithful and under the developing circumstances, the Ecumenical Patriarchate continues, in its ecumenical diakonia, to remain an essential part of the European dimension. Beyond the ideological orientation of each of you; beyond each individual's personal conviction, metaphysical or not, we kindly ask you to accept the readiness of the Ecumenical Patriarchate to support you in your efforts for European unification, for a Europe which will exist not only for itself, but for the good of all of humanity.

We wish to conclude with a prayer which we Orthodox

direct to the Prince of Peace, especially during the period of Great Lent:

> Heavenly King, strengthen our faith,
> reconcile the nations and give peace to world.

Tolerance and the Integrity of One's Own Faith are not Mutually Exclusive

GEORGE CAREY

The author is Archbishop of Canterbury and head of the Anglican Communion

I, like many other religious leaders, am deeply indebted to Hans Küng and to the Parliament of the World's Religions for their work in seeking to articulate a 'global ethic'. As he has stated on a number of occasions, we live in a world where the role of the religions must not be underestimated. 'For,' as he writes, 'there can be no peace among the nations without peace among the religions.'

That view, so long neglected, is now being canvassed by many students of statecraft, and the significance of religion, for good or ill, is being recognized by many politicians.

In the search for global harmony, those of us who are religious leaders have a crucial role to play. We live in a fractured and confused world where spokesmen of the different faiths can, all too frequently, be seen to be adding to the disharmony. Our job, rather, should be to model the ways in which those of the different faith traditions can learn to live alongside one another, exercising tolerance whilst retaining our integrity.

On a personal level this is something I have come to appreciate much more deeply since becoming Archbishop of Canterbury. Nationally I and my predecessors have come to act in certain respects as a kind of 'honest broker' on behalf of the other faith communities of our country in their relationships with its 'Establishment'. At worst this could be seen as a kind of paternalism but, at its best, it results in mutual benefit and the growth of real respect. One of the things I appreciate greatly is the opportunity I have to meet with their leaders, to discuss subjects of common concern, and to speak out, at times, on their behalf. Likewise, internationally, both through my travels, and from the correspondence I receive, I have come to see more clearly the damage that can be done through religious disharmony, and the very real benefits that can arise when a minority Christian community's integrity is respected and where true tolerance is maintained by the majority community of another faith.

In this brief essay, then, I want to explore further those concepts of tolerance and integrity and to suggest practical ways in which we can build the former without compromising the latter. Let me treat each in turn:

Genuine tolerance should be based upon a true acceptance of one another

Let me make one thing clear from the start. Tolerance is not to be confused with indifference. When Baroness Wootton declared that, 'People are tolerant only about things they do not really care about', she was describing accurately what many people mean when they talk about being tolerant. But such 'tolerance' is not true tolerance at all. It is merely indifference.

 True tolerance, on the other hand, exists where people disagree markedly with one another and yet recognize, and uphold, the right of each other to hold differing opinions. Indeed true toleration can only be exercised when we come close enough to each other to share in genuine encounter in what Americans love to describe as 'eyeball to eyeball contact'. Such contact happens all too infrequently in many parts of the world. Faith communities become isolated and mistrust grows as a result. But there are ways to break these barriers down. Let me suggest three practical steps for fostering genuine tolerance:

(a) *Examining our own faith tradition critically*. One of the features of the late twentieth century is the growth of fundamentalism in a wide variety of faith traditions. One common characteristic of all such movements is a refusal to look critically at themselves. They are right, whilst all others are wrong. That is, of course, a mark, very often, of immaturity and insecurity, but it is a very powerful force nonetheless. It results in a culture in which tolerance has little or no chance of growing. To counter such tendencies, which are present, even if only in embryonic form, in most of us, we need to be honest about our own shortcomings, and not pretend we have an exclusive right to hold the moral high ground. Within the Christian tradition this means acknowledging much that has shamed our high ideals down the centuries, whether in the Crusades, or in the failure to stand up to the evils of Nazi power, or, most recently, in the tragedies of Bosnia and Rwanda. But it is not just Christians who have those stories to tell. Similar ones, sadly, belong to all of the major faith traditions, and wherever we look in the world – India, Pakistan, the Middle East, the Far East and elsewhere – we find the same instinct to demand tolerance for ourselves whilst refusing it to others. Through acknowledging this common tendency we will discover that our eyes will focus less sharply on the perceived failings of others and true tolerance will have a chance to grow.

(b) *Fostering good education and training*. It is only comparatively recently that British school-children have begun to be taught about faith communities other than the dominant Christian one. This development has been overlong in coming to this country, and it is one whose results in terms of greater community understanding will not be known for many years to come. But education is essential if we wish to see change taking place. Religious and cultural differences can cause us to shrink back in fear, and strangeness is often difficult to face.

One part of education which we can address as religious leaders is in seeking ways to inform and educate our local congregations. However, that will only happen if the educators are educated first themselves. Christian clergy, imams, rabbis and others exercising leadership roles need to have their horizons extended beyond the boundaries of their own faith community. For instance, in how many of our theological colleges, departments of theology and *yeshivas* is theology taught in such a way as to give full weight to this 'interfaith' dimension? When studying, say, the doctrine of God, it should no longer be taught as if the widely differing perceptions of Judaism, Hinduism, Islam and Christianity did not exist. I have argued elsewhere that those training at our theological colleges should be exposed to the teachings of two other faiths during their time at them. Such a pattern should, I believe, be replicated elsewhere as a serious contribution to the growth of understanding and tolerance.

(c) *Acting together on community issues.* Another way in which barriers can be broken down between people is through the process of working together for a common cause. Often this will start at the level of local believers meeting together, sharing their common concerns and addressing issues that are of mutual importance. For instance a concern for the local environment is something which can evoke a united response without any group feeling compromised by their involvement with others.

An English example of this kind of co-operation is the Inner Cities Religious Council. This is supported jointly by the Government and the Church of England, and brings together representatives of many different faiths to focus on the needs of inner-city communities, discuss them with Government, initiate practical projects, and stimulate community involvement. Where words and doctrines can easily divide us, action unifies.

But, building on that kind of experience, true tolerance also seeks to identify those areas which can be shared, even if the pain one religious group feels is not shared by the other. I think of a situation in the city of Bradford where, in the city hospital, patients from minority religious groups, notably Muslims, felt unable to get spiritual support in the predominantly Christian ethos of medical care. The Christian chaplain, a Nigerian, who was sensitive to their needs, brought the matter to the attention of the chaplaincy committee. That committee empathized at such a depth in this matter that the needs of those concerned were taken up with the kind of energy one would expect if the problem at stake had been one which the committee shared personally. One result has been the provision of a room in the hospital specifically for worship, which is now being used by members of the different communities. Such genuine toleration is born of real involvement which feels the pain of another.

Many other examples could be added to this list of practical ways of building tolerance. For the Christian, the impetus for such involvement springs from our Lord's command to 'love our neighbour as ourselves'. Such neighbourliness begins when we recognize the true humanity of others and seek to enter into their experiences. That is the source of true tolerance.

But, as I stated earlier, alongside such tolerance there must be:

Proper understanding of the integrity and uniqueness of faith

Devout people resent being told that essentially all religions are the same. At a time when some have seen culture as being all-determinative, it is a mistake to assert that all the different faiths are only attempts to describe the One Reality from the background of a variety of cultural contexts. The Christian theologian and philosopher Professor John Hick is well known for his argument that all faiths are essentially 'parochial'. Moreover he argues that only when we are fully prepared to recognize this will the imperialism behind a great deal of missionary expansion cease and greater harmony between religions begin.

I am not alone in disagreeing with his basic argument.

Professor Hick's starting point is that, without shedding the ancient doctrine of the incarnation of God in Jesus, the Christian faith cannot authentically participate in dialogue because it will always assume the fundamental superiority of its own world-view. In his most recent writings he has argued that Christians should see the incarnation as a 'metaphor' which may be held in tension with other metaphors of belief in other faiths. However, it is a mistake to reduce our great faith traditions to a matter of cultural conformity. A variation of this approach seeks to shrug away the differences between the faiths as something that will be resolved with greater education and greater understanding between the faith traditions. That, too, I believe to be a vain hope which will prevent us from tackling the real issues head on.

Nowhere is the subject of integrity more sharply focused than in the question of the importance of the missionary imperative to a faith tradition. Whilst in some religions it is absent, or at least viewed as an 'optional extra', for Christians, Muslims and some others it lies close to the heart of their self-understanding. Even if all aggressive and improper forms of proselytism are eschewed, including, of course, any kind of cultural imperialism, Christians seeking to be faithful to their beliefs cannot, with integrity, neglect their calling to express those beliefs and to share them with others.

This can, at times, be a difficult position to hold whilst remaining deeply committed to fostering harmony amongst the religions.

To be true to myself I need to say explicitly that for me, Jesus Christ is the compelling centre of faith, the final revelation of God, and that it is my desire to offer him to all. I see no reason to hide this fact and I have never done so. Does this mean, therefore, there can be no dialogue and no peace between the religions? Of course not. I do not accept that there is a basic incompatibility between the religions of the world that defies dialogue and the sharing of common values, leading on to the espousal of a global ethic. The crucial question relates to the 'language' and 'manner' of the relationship. Although I am clear in my conviction that Jesus Christ is for all, the Person I follow is one who 'came to serve, not to be served'; He is one who cared for and loved others. Therefore I am compelled to come to others, not with an arrogant message of 'follow or be damned', but with an invitation to 'taste and see how good the Lord is'.

But invitations are a two-way thing. If I go with an invitation to someone else of another faith, I am equally compelled to listen to his story of faith and renewal. I must stand open to be challenged by his story and his experiences. From personal experience I can say that as a result of such frank and generous encounters, a greater understanding of another faith results, together with deep friendships which sees the other as a brother and sister. We may not agree about the answers, but we do share the urgency to do something about the questions that life poses.

Such an approach is, I believe, the way to hold these two imperatives in a productive tension.

In my experience, the missionary drive explicit in Christianity and some other faiths is entirely compatible with good will and harmony among the different faiths. Indeed, a willingness to share our faith in this way with others will lead us into a deepening appreciation of the richness of the traditions with which we are unfamiliar, and can be done with full integrity.

The vision behind the Declaration of the Religions for a Global Ethic is twofold: the fundamental unity of the human family and the potential of all faiths to make a distinctive contribution toward world peace. That is something to celebrate. I believe that we are at a moment in world history when men and women of good will can make an unparalleled contribution towards the peace among the nations. We who are leaders must set the pace. We must with integrity seek a true tolerance based upon a commitment to each other and espouse policies which will transcend all forms of behaviour that create hatred, resentment and divison.

In Agreement with Christianity

JOSEPH BERNARDIN

*The author is Archbishop of Chicago and a cardinal of
the Roman Catholic Church*

As the preparations for the 1993 Parliament of the World's
Religions were drawing to a close, I received the text of *A
Global Ethic*. This two-part work included, 'The Principles of
a Global Ethic', crafted by Dr Hans Küng out of consultations
that he held with scholars at the University of Tübingen and
elsewhere, and the 'Declaration of a Global Ethic', a summary
of the longer work condensed by the trustees of the Council for
a Parliament of the World's Religions. *A Global Ethic* set out
the hypothesis that significant agreement on common ethical
norms already exists among the religions of the world. The
Assembly of Religious and Spiritual Leaders at the 1993
Parliament in Chicago strongly endorsed the two-part work.
To stress the provisional nature of the dialogue, it was retitled,
Toward a Global Ethic, an Initial Declaration.

I recall my first reaction on reading the early draft. Of
course, the religions of the world will agree on common ethical
norms. I also recall my second reaction, which was a question.
'What is the content of that agreement? How far can such a
document go?' It seemed that a tension existed between the
intuitive sense that the religious traditions of the human family
should agree on ethics, and the intellectual sense that we do
not really know the content or extent of this agreement. A
person reading *Toward a Global Ethic* encounters at once a
problem of perspective. Is the glass half-empty, or half-full?

Initially, I found the glass half-empty. What struck me first
in the text were its omissions. It is expected that an interfaith

text cannot go as far as I, as a Catholic bishop, would wish it to go – for example, with regard to respect for every human life. So, on my first reading, I longed for the text to develop its points more fully. Yet, the document offered a tone of hopefulness.

A second reading revealed a real wealth of agreement. The full realization of the four irrevocable directives would be the morality of the Ten Commandments. Thoroughly Christian, it is also thoroughly Buddhist, thoroughly Jewish, thoroughly Zoroastrian. Said another way, it is thoroughly human. All people of good will, whether religious or not, can find challenge in this text to adopt behaviours which will build up human society rather than tear it down.

So after thorough study, I signed the text. And others did also, nearly 250, almost the entire Assembly of Religious and Spiritual Leaders. While not a representative body in any manner, this group of serious, thoughtful, and committed individuals acted together to send a message to the entire human family. That message said three things:

1. We believe a common ethic is possible.
2. We have begun an experiment to find both its core and its limits.
3. We invite all people, whether religious or not, to join us.

I fully endorse this goal, and I offer the following points as constructive criticism to help it on its way.

An experiment

First, the global ethic is an experiment that is presently at the point of hypothesis. It seemed to me and the other 250 persons who endorsed the initial declaration that there is sufficient convergence among the religions to claim the existence of a global ethic. Now the task is to develop the content and extent of that ethic as a thesis which the religions of the world can officially consider. If the thesis can be successfully defended, not merely in an interfaith assembly but also in an actual dialogue among the religions about the document's contents, then it will emerge as an authentic transcultural ethic. This would be a significant contribution to the human family.

However, the project has not yet matured to the stage of being authentically transcultural. It can do so, but first certain issues of content must be raised and answered in the dialogue. Each religion will have different views about these issues. I only speak for myself as a bishop of the Catholic Church. For the global ethic to be a viable thesis, it will need to address many issues. I will suggest only a few.

1. What is the basis for morality? Is interdependence sufficient? Or does the human family need first to recognize the Creator? Are human rights and responsibilities consequences of creation? The declaration comes close to a natural-law formulation, but this could be more specific.

2. Can ethics exist apart from faith? How are faith and morals related? Christianity understands these as two parts of an integral whole. How can this wholistic approach be accomplished for the global ethic?

3. How are we to address the need for systemic change of unjust structures in society? The initial global ethic is highly individualistic, which is fine as far as this goes. But there are some ethical issues that belong to the social structure, and justice must be applied there. Also, the global ethic does not address the mediating structures which join the individual to the community. Governments, corporations, religious and not-for-profit groups, businesses, trade unions – all have a role to play in the fabric of human society. Ethical governments, ethical corporations, ethical religious organizations, ethical businesses and trade groups – all can make a powerful contribution to the human community.

These are only a few issues that need development in the document. To advance the dialogue, I would like to address them from a Christian viewpoint and then offer some comments on the content of the four irrevocable directives.

What is the basis for morality?

For Christians, ethics is part of the human vocation towards eternal life in the glory of heaven. The human person, in freedom, is obliged to follow the moral law, to do good and avoid evil. This freedom is the evidence of our creation in God's image and likeness (*Gaudium et spes*, 17).

Christianity brings to the conversation the insight that human nature is wounded. Whether we use the term original sin or not, human beings are subject to errors and inclined to evil in the exercise of their freedom (*Catechism of the Catholic Church*, 1714).

The moral life, then, as Christians understand it, is fully possible only through God's grace. Though created in God's image, we require divine help to overcome this wound and to mature in God's likeness. We must set our hearts on the higher things. For Christians, the vision of this life is found in the Scriptures, especially in the Beatitudes (Matthew 5.1–12). The dialogue could be served if other religious leaders would point to the sacred texts of their tradition, which lift their vision to the higher things. In this way, we could begin to see the convergence in content which would make a global ethic possible.

Can ethics exist apart from faith?

We need to dialogue about the source of authority for a global ethic. I subscribed to the document because of its correspondence to my own religion. I trust that the other participants did the same. But again, the dialogue would benefit from an articulation of the sources of morality. Christians understand that morality is grounded in the object, the intention, and the circumstances of human action (*Catechism of the Catholic Church*, 1754). This is a weakness in the Declaration. As the Muslim delegates at the Assembly of Religious and Spiritual Leaders noted when they challenged the term non-violence and asked that it be nuanced to non-aggression, circumstance is an important component in moral judgment. Circumstance also includes the consequences of an action. The Declaration treats intention in a way by calling for a change in consciousness. But Christians look for an articulation of objective morality as well as subjective.

To know what objects of ethical action are truly good and not evil, one must know something of the virtues. All the historic world religions teach about virtue. A convergence here will be necessary for the global ethic to function effectively as more than a least common denominator, although even that would help society. As the bishop of a local church where the daily newspaper carries a tally sheet on the front page of the number of children killed with guns, I would praise God if even a lowest-common-denominator ethic could be achieved in Chicago. However, a global ethic can do much more. One important role for religion is to challenge the consciences of peoples and societies.

That is why it is important for contemporary society to hear the behaviours condemned in the Declaration. Today, we sometimes tend to avoid words like 'sin'. Yet, there are certain human behaviours that are damaging and even abhorrent! The *Catechism of the Catholic Church* defines sin as:

> An offence against reason, truth and right conscience; it is failure in genuine love for God and neighbour caused by a perverse attachment to certain goods. It wounds the nature of man and injures human solidarity. It has been defined as 'an utterance, a deed, or a desire contrary to the eternal law' (1849).

If we want society to avoid certain behaviours, we must be

honest where these behaviours come from. Do other religions have an articulation of 'capital' or 'root' sins? It would be instructive to know if pride, avarice, envy, wrath, lust, gluttony and sloth have parallel teachings in the other religions.

The need for systemic change

Similarly, sin has an effect on the mediating institutions I mentioned above. We are not isolated in this world.

> Sins give rise to social situations and institutions that are contrary to the divine goodness. 'Structures of sin' are the expression and effect of personal sins. They also lead their victims to do evil. In an analogous sense, they constitute a 'social sin' (*Catechism of the Catholic Church*, 1869).

Regarding the mediating structures between the individual and the global community, one of the contributions that Christianity can make to this interreligious dialogue concerns social thought. Modern papal social teaching, which was inaugurated at the same time as the first Parliament of the World's Religions, has developed over the past 100 years. In many ways, this social teaching is a foundation on which the Second Vatican Council's teaching on ecumenism, inter-religious dialogue and religious liberty is built. This papal social teaching states that:

> The human person needs to live in society. Society is not for him an extraneous addition but a requirement of his nature. Through the exchange with others, mutual service and dialogue with his brethren, man develops his potential; he thus responds to his vocation (*Catechism of the Catholic Church*, 1879).

Allow me to raise up certain points from this Christian view.

(*a*) The first and primary component of society is the family. That is why the Catholic Church teaches that the marriage of man and woman is the fundamental social unit and instrument. Here in the United States we are finding that a society will only be as strong as the marriages and families of that society. Marriage and family are the basic building blocks of the common good.

(*b*) The common good has three elements: respect for the human person, the requirement of social well-being and development, and peace. Because of this, one of the mediating structures the global ethic needs to consider more fully is the political community. The responsibility for fostering the common good belongs to the political community in a pre-eminent way. This constitutes what papal social teaching calls the progress of peoples.

(*c*) One of the strengths of *Toward a Global Ethic* is its insistence on responsibility. There is also the need to recognize both individual responsibility and responsibility at the level of the mediating institutions for participation by people in fostering the common good. All of this presupposes the principle of subsidiarity.

(*d*) Another component to consider is human solidarity. In the United States, as a result of the US Catholic bishops' Campaign for Human Development, many people of good will have come to know the words of Pope Paul VI, 'If you want peace, work for justice!'

Socio-economic problems can be resolved only with the help of all forms of solidarity: solidarity of the poor among themselves, between rich and poor, of workers among themselves, between employers and employees, among nations and peoples. International solidarity is a requirement of the moral order; world peace depends in part upon this (*Catechism of the Catholic Church*, 1941).

The four irrevocable directives

Let us turn now to the specifics of the four irrevocable directives, which I earlier described as the morality of the Ten Commandments. It is very important that each religion consider the content of each directive and its correspondence to the content of its own traditional religious teaching. It is here that the human person seeks objective morality. For us to be able to establish ethical agreement, it is important to know what each of the historic world religions holds as the content of the four irrevocable directives.

(a) You shall not kill

> The Catholic Church holds that the deliberate murder of an innocent person is gravely contrary to the dignity of the human being, the golden rule, and the holiness of the Creator. The law forbidding it is universally valid: it obliges each and everyone, always and everywhere (*Catechism of the Catholic Church*, 2261).

That being said, I must note that Christian tradition includes the possibility of legitimate defence. This was also voiced on the floor of the Assembly by several Muslim delegates. The Fifth Commandment forbids direct and intentional killing. It forbids infanticide, fratricide, parricide and murder of a spouse. It forbids abortion. The positive command, 'have respect for life', requires a definition of life. The Catholic Christian tradition holds that life begins at conception, and, from conception, a human being must be recognized as having the rights of a person, among which is the inviolable right of every innocent being to life (Congregation for the Doctrine of the Faith, *Donum Vitae* I, 1).

Respect for life is multifaceted. During the past eleven years, I have articulated the need for a consistent ethic of life. I have pointed out that all life-issues are distinct, but also interrelated. This includes euthanasia, the topic of my own major presentation at the 1993 Parliament. Such an ethic also includes consideration of suicide, capital punishment, domestic violence, and respect for persons who are disabled. Having respect for life includes having respect for health as well as respect for persons in the face of scientific research and technology. It includes a respect for bodily integrity, which is affronted by kidnapping, hostage-taking and terrorism. It includes torture and, especially, forced amputation, mutilations and sterilizations.

The Fifth Commandment also calls upon us to safeguard peace, to avoid war, and to resolve conflict by peaceful means. One of the most important calls heard at the Parliament was the call to establish some means to mediate religiously-based conflict.

(b) You shall not commit adultery

Catholic Christian teaching on chastity begins with an understanding of creation. God created the human race as male and female.

> Sexuality affects all aspects of the human person in the unity of one's body and soul. It especially concerns affectivity, the capacity to love and to procreate, and in a more general way the aptitude for forming bonds of communion with others (*Catechism of the Catholic Church*, 2332).

In the marriage rite, the Church prays for the groom that he will recognize the bride as his equal and heir with him to the life of grace (*Roman Ritual*, The Rite of Marriage, 33). A basic fact of creation is that all human generation proceeds from the union of man and woman. For men and women to enter into a life of equal partnership, each must maintain the integrity of the other. They must reject any thoughts, words, or actions that reduce the other person to the position of an object.

Hence, chastity is of primary importance as we consider the Sixth Commandment, since it is the means to self-mastery which makes the gift of self possible.

The Sixth Commandment calls for men and women to live lives of friendship. Hostility between the genders is destructive to human society. Friendship cannot grow when one person is treating another as an object. Only when people are accorded their rightful dignity can there be the opportunity for the self-giving of friendship. Chastity is the constant refusal to turn another person into an object.

No consideration of sexuality would be complete without attention to the offences against chastity. Rape and prostitution are clear examples of acts that violate the dignity of the human person. Less clear to society are pornography and homosexual genital activity, which also violate the natural law. I am a member of the Religious Alliance Against Pornography, an inter-religious group working to challenge the contemporary notion of pornography as a victimless crime.

> Pornography ... does grave injury to the dignity of its participants (actors, vendors, the public), since each one becomes an object of base pleasure and illicit profit for others. It immerses all involved in the illusion of a fantasy world. It is a grave offence. Civil authorities should prevent the production and distribution of pornographic materials (*Catechism of the Catholic Church*, 2354).

Homosexuality is another highly controversial issue today. In a recent videotaped pastoral statement to teenagers in the Archdiocese of Chicago I spoke of two critical aspects of this issue.

First is the matter of discrimination:

> The number of men and women who have deep-seated homosexual tendencies is not negligible. They do not choose their homosexual condition; for most of them it is a

trial. They must be accepted with respect, compassion, and sensitivity. Every sign of unjust discrimination in their regard should be avoided (*Catechism of the Catholic Church*, 2358).

Secondly, Catholic tradition makes a distinction between a homosexual orientation and homosexual genital acts. Catholic Christian teaching holds that the sexual union exists to achieve the twofold end of marriage, the good of the spouses themselves and the transmission of life. These two ends are integral and cannot be separated. Therefore, any sexual activity outside of heterosexual marriage is illicit.

I said above that a society is only as strong as the marriages and families in it. So, some attention must be paid to offences against the dignity of marriage. Of these, adultery is foremost. In fact, it is this sin that the Decalogue names and under which church tradition collects all other sexual sins. Divorce, so prevalent in the world today, does violence to the family and is especially difficult on children. Free unions, trial marriages and the so-called 'open marriages' all erode the institution of marriage and have a profound and negative effect on society as a whole. Polygamy, incest, sexual abuse of children or adolescents are all violations of the dignity of the human person. As such they cannot be permitted.

(c) You shall not steal

The Seventh Commandment of the Decalogue is a positive teaching about the practices of justice and charity regarding material things. In particular, this commandment is concerned with human labour.

Catholic teaching considers the ethics of material wealth from the viewpoint of the universal destiny or purpose of goods. Even though we understand that people have a right to private property, that right is not unlimited. It is limited because even within it there is a universal destiny: goods must serve all humanity. Personal, commercial or governmental purposes must never lead to an enslavement of people. Slavery is forbidden.

Also, Catholic teaching, looking from the vantage point of the universal destiny of goods, requires the consideration of both inter-generational and environmental equity. The dominion over the natural kingdom granted to humanity by God must be one of stewardship.

While there is much consideration of economic and social development in contemporary thought, labour itself is for the development of human beings. In labour, a human being both gives and receives. It is therefore a model of the social order.

(d) You shall not bear false witness against your neighbour

Saint Paul, in the Letter to the Romans, teaches that God is truth and that the people of God are called to live in the truth. Further, the Gospel of John reveals that Jesus, the revelation of God, is the Truth in which Christians are to live.

As a bishop of the Catholic Church, my first question regarding the matter of truth is its source. How do we humans come to know the truth? While an interfaith document cannot be expected to reach consensus on this point, nevertheless an identification of each religion's approach to truth could strengthen the force of any subsequent agreement on content.

Truth, in a religious sense, makes a claim on its disciples. The enforcement of a global ethic will largely come from the claims to truth that an individual or religion sees in the document. Ethics requires a person to live in the truth. This again raises my earlier question of the relationship of faith to morals.

This particular commandment deals with living in the truth and bearing witness to the truth. The claim of truth requires testimony. If the content of a global ethic is judged to be true, then one must give witness to it. Within this is the motive for a religion to use the global ethic. Christians will not use it because the Parliament of the World's Religions endorsed it, less still because I personally endorsed it. Christians will use a global ethic because they see the truth in it. Their commitment to truth is the motive for both endorsing the ethic and putting it into practice. An interfaith exploration of the motive for such a declaration could also strengthen the document.

In terms of the content of the Eighth Commandment, how may truth be offended? Sins of false witness and perjury, defamation of reputation, rash judgment, detraction and calumny are all offences against truth.

> Lying is the most direct offence against the truth. To lie is to speak or act against the truth in order to lead into error someone who has the right to know the truth. By injuring one's relation to truth and to his or her neighbour, a lie offends against the fundamental relation of a person's word to the Lord (*Catechism of the Catholic Church*, 2483).

Respect for the truth requires a right to the communication of the truth. While such a right exists in natural law, it is not unconditional. The good and safety of others, respect for privacy, and the common good are important reasons for being silent. Another is the prevention of scandal. There needs to be a balance between the requirements of the common good and individual rights. Either extreme does violence to the preservation of truth (*Catechism of the Catholic Church*, 2491). It is important for the global ethic to consider the boundaries of this and other human rights.

In any study of truth the communications media need special consideration. The media have an enormous role in the transmission of information and in the promotion and formation of culture. The media should see themselves in the service of culture. Ethical media are a tremendous power for good in society. Unethical media have a similar destructive power. Individual journalists, communication companies and the mass media, as well as civil authorities – all have a responsibility to serve truth and not offend against justice and charity.

Another vital form of communication of truth is art.

Commonly, we think of issues of truth in terms of words. But returning to what I said above about the need to view ethics within a larger vision of virtue, a consideration of truth should also consider art, especially sacred art.

> Indeed, art is a distinctively human form of expression. Beyond the search for the necessities of life which is common to all living creatures, art is a form of practical wisdom, uniting knowledge and skill to give form to the truth of reality in a language accessible to sight or hearing (*Catechism of the Catholic Church*, 2501).

It would be a very interesting dialogue, indeed, if the religions of the world, besides identifying the sacred texts that instruct them on virtue, were also to share the sacred art which conveys the same message.

While I have tried to be specific, this short reflection by no means exhausts what Catholic Christianity says on each of these topics. While an interfaith document cannot be expected to reach full conformity with comprehensive Catholic teaching, a high degree of agreement is possible on many particulars among the historic world religions. I am encouraged by how easy it has been to dialogue with this document. It corresponds well with Christianity. What is needed is to become as specific as the dialogue will permit. This will not be easy. But if this experiment succeeds, the 1993 Parliament of the World's Religions will have given a special gift to humanity. May God will it to be so!

The Ethic of Peace

PAULO EVARISTO ARNS

*The author is Archbishop of São Paulo and a cardinal of
the Roman Catholic Church*

The following text is the speech of thanks which I gave on
being awarded the Niwano Peace Prize. So it is not a direct
commentary on the Parliament of the World's Religions'
Declaration on a Global Ethic. But any reader who compares
my speech with the Declaration will be able to note the deep
parallels in the basic concerns and in individual problems. I
myself was not able to take part in the Parliament of the
World's Religions, although Nikko Niwano had invited me to
speak at this Parliament in his name. But I support with all my
heart the cause of the Parliament which is so impressively
expressed in its Declaration. The following text will make this
support quite specific at many points.

With the end of what was called the Cold War and the
constant threat of the use of nuclear arms among the world's
most powerful nations, we felt that now we would know peace
in our time. But since all the symbols of the Iron Curtain, the
Berlin Wall have fallen, we have seen a world that faces
violence and war continuously on the local level.

What is peace?

We are now forced to ask ourselves: What is peace? Is it the
absence of world-wide ideological or economic divisions? Is it
a time of prosperity when poverty has been overcome? I do not
think so. Peace is not the absence of war; it is not economic

prosperity; it is not even worldwide majority rule. Peace is a transcendent gift that becomes a reality of daily life when it becomes a habit of each human being.

When I read Nichiko Niwano's book, *My Father, My Teacher*, I was impressed by his words about habit and the Lotus Sutra. He quotes the philosopher Henri Amiel, who says: To learn new habits is everything, for it is to reach the substance of life. Life is but a tissue of habits.

This is as important in the Christian tradition as Nichiko Niwano says it is for Buddhists. Our holiest theologians – whom we call saints – would agree with the Flower Garland Sutra (Avatamsaka Sutra) that merely hearing many teachings cannot rid the mind of delusions unless it is accompanied by practical action. Repeated practical actions result in habit. In Christian vocabulary habit is virtue, habit is the way to peace and to holiness.

Jesus, the centre of our Christian religion, showed us that the most profoundly creative way to overcome enemies is to make them our friends. But this involves a series of painful acts: a constant decision never to achieve our goals by destroying or humiliating others.

We Catholics call this constant effort to build peace the practice of the spiritual and corporal works of mercy. We begin by bearing wrongs patiently and forgiving all injuries. These habits (virtues) help us to help others: comforting the sorrowful, counselling the doubtful and helping the ignorant and the erring to discover and love the path to life.

At the same time we believe in other habits that guarantee peace:

- feeding the hungry;
- giving drink to the thirsty;
- clothing the naked;
- visiting the imprisoned;
- sheltering the homeless;
- visiting the ill and
- burying the dead with reverence.

When I was a child we could all recite these works of mercy by heart. But it was not always that these essential works of our religion became habits. Nichiko Niwano is right. If our teaching leads to practice, practice will instil good habits in the mind, and these habits are a powerful force, a second nature that transforms our way of living.

The dedication of the religions to peace

If all the religions of the world would dedicate themselves to this type of practical education, the way to peace would be guaranteed. Peace, especially world peace, is too important to be left only to the politicians! Peacemaking is a lifelong effort that depends on multitudes of people. Every religion has to form and educate persons who are just in their personal dealings, because without this conversion of persons there can be no real peace. But we also need to influence on the social and institutional levels.

We often behave in a certain way because we are reflecting the social groups and institutions to which we belong. For this reason we have to support the institutions and movements that work for justice and struggle, to change all those that are unjust and lead to conflict and social unrest. Religious people must realize that peacemaking is not an optional commitment. We are called to be dedicated peacemakers exactly because we are religious.

When others respond with anger in the midst of nationalist, racial or ideological conflicts, we have to take time to see beneath the surface and to recognize that conflicts are never overcome by violence. The important events of history are the thousands of humble actions that heal and reconcile.

Each one of us has to make an act of faith in the power of our own words and acts to foster a climate of peace. Every day we have an opportunity to speak words of forgiveness and reconciliation, to act in ways that overcome hostility and prejudice.

We believe that the mystery of unconditional love is the central condition of peace. Why is unconditional love a mystery? We human beings always condition our love. We are good to those who are good to us, forgive those who forgive us, speak well of those who speak well of us. But this attitude does not create peace.

Peace means to love our enemies, forgive those who do not forgive us and do good to the spiteful, the liars, the prejudiced, the violent. This is a gift from the real Wisdom. Only unconditional love can create the conditions for peace. For Christians this means to be holy, to live divine life on earth. If I understood well, this is the wisdom and compassion of which Buddha speaks. True wisdom enables us to see the essential qualities of all things in this world. If we are possessed of such wisdom, we cannot help practising rightly in everything we do. We cannot do wrong even if we are deceived or led into temptation by others. The more people who can acquire such wisdom, the brighter, more peaceful, and richer society will become. Arnold Toynbee once said: 'When an historian one thousand years from now writes about the twentieth century, he will surely be more interested in the interpenetration which occurred for the first time between Christianity and Buddhism than in the conflict between the ideologies of democracy and communism.' These words deeply impressed me as the words of a man who clearly sees what will really move history and be meaningful among the many things that mankind will leave for its descendants.

Towards a just economic order

I have always believed that our actions for peace, even the most humble, contribute to the climate which supports political decisions that involve the lives of millions. To be peacemakers we must care for all we meet and never, ever, use people to reach our own goals, no matter how noble they are.

For this reason, in the almost two and a half decades that I have been Archbishop of São Paulo, I have tried to encourage those of all faiths to work for peace through small gestures that are possible for all of us. In 1971 I made an appeal on the radio and in the archdiocesan newspaper to involve as many people as possible in solving the problems of those who live on the outskirts, the periphery, of our city.

This programme was called 'Operation Periphery'. All the religious of the city were called to send as many members as possible to work with the people in the poorest neigh-bourhoods. Operation Periphery became a movement that involved numerous Catholics from the centre of the city. It has been a great consolation to me that many future priests who dreamed of being responsible for the city's largest and most prestigious parishes in the 1960s saw their colleagues of the 1970s and 1980s choosing to work in chapels and community centres far from the city centre. The option for the poor that became the heart of the church in Latin America at the international assembly at Medellin in 1968 began to penetrate the way of the Christians of São Paulo. Operation Periphery was not a simple programme but became a movement, a way of thinking, a way of life. It was one more little step on the way to peace.

Operation Periphery led the Christians of São Paulo to get to know the millions of inhabitants who lived in poor housing on the outskirts of the city and had to travel from five to seven hours a day to get back and forth to their jobs. This knowledge, plus an intensive formation programme in our religious principles, led us to invite all the participants to organize themselves in small religious communities based on the union of families that lived on the same street in the same neighbourhood. In a short time, five thousand women and men became 'preachers' of our religious principles, and they invited their neighbours to come together, deepen their faith and face their common problems, spiritual and material.

These communities worked to have better education for their children; better transportation; better health conditions (water, sewerage, hospitals, garbage collections). They worked together to better their homes and to build simple houses for newcomers arriving in São Paulo. All of this activity led the inhabitants of these poor areas to see other needs they had not been conscious of before.

Local centres of human rights

It soon became clear to all those involved that it was very dangerous to be poor. Not only were the poor more liable to disease and to the destruction of their homes by floods, but they were looked on by society as being potential criminals. If something was stolen, the police arrested the poorest person in the vicinity. If there was a riot at a football game, the police beat the worst-dressed of the men.

For this reason, the communities founded, in each neighbourhood, a Centre for the Defence of Human Rights. In these centres local lawyers or law students, with the help of their colleagues from the centre of the city, tried to defend the innocent poor from a great number of accusations. They also defended those 'guilty' of stealing food for their children, or money for medicine, so that these people would not be jailed for long periods. After a certain time, these centres also became responsible for social education programmes. Topics of interest to all – such as the new constitution – were translated into simple terms and drawings so that the whole population could understand what they were voting for and what was most important for their futures.

At the same time that all of this was occurring on the periphery of the city, some of our most famous jurists and intellectuals came together to work for justice and peace on a broader level. They defended persons and groups that were being unjustly persecuted for political reasons. They acted on the national and international level.

All of this work led an inter-religious group to the necessity of having a special programme for refugees from the southern cone of South America. Many people had been arrested and tortured for political reasons. They arrived in São Paulo with their families and under the protection of the United Nations. We had to help them find housing, jobs, schools for their children. When they were ill we arranged hospitals, and when they were worried about the families they left behind, we tried to get news for them.

All of this work in defence of human rights led an inter-religious group to see the necessity of documenting all the illegal political imprisonments and torture that had been happening continuously in Brazil for over twenty years. With considerable danger to themselves, many lawyers and their collaborators xeroxed all the official judicial trials with the extensive descriptions of false arrests and torture.

A resumé was published in Portuguese in Brazil and in English in the United States. I had to be personally responsible for the Brazilian edition, because none of our publishing houses wanted to take on the responsibility!

São Paulo has always suffered from an urban poverty that condemns many poor families literally to live on the street. For many decades religious people have gone on to the streets in the middle of the night, taking clothes, blankets and hot soup or coffee to the street dwellers.

As time went on and inflation and economic recession caused more and more unemployment, it was necessary for more Christians to involve themselves in services to the group we call the 'street sufferers'. In some places the people come together at noon to make a hot meal where everything is shared. Lawyers help to defend these people from attacks by the police. Everyone knows they exist, but the population does not want to see them. If they are under a bridge they are driven away. If they sleep in the archways of public buildings they are driven away again. I am ashamed to say that many Catholics do not like to see the poor sleeping in the doorways of our churches!

But, more and more people are beginning to understand that these families are the victims of our political and economic system. We have to work for familial integration and not to increase their sufferings by blaming the victims for the crime!

Not only the 'street sufferers' but many workers in São Paulo are homeless because the rents are increased more rapidly than the salaries. Also, in São Paulo, as in Tokyo, the price of land is exorbitant. Millions live in poor housing on the outskirts of the city. But the cost of transportation leads the very poor to look for any kind of precarious housing nearer to their jobs, often found in the centre of the city.

Thousands of these families go to live in shacks on the sides of hills or near rivers and highways. These places are known all over the world as *favelas*, a certain kind of slum. Church groups have worked to make many of these places more habitable. With the help of friends from all over the world electricity, running water, sewerage and paved streets have been brought to some *favelas*.

Thousands of other families live in old abandoned houses. Where one family lived thirty years ago, today there are twenty or thirty. Many church groups work with these families that are living in situations much worse than those in many *favelas*. For this reason, the church in São Paulo has sponsored housing as a priority during the last two decades. Our families cannot fulfil their mission if they do not have the spiritual and material conditions to do so.

Health and medical care

The material conditions of life have led us to promote ministries or services to our enormous population. It is only the spiritual that can give us the continuous energy we need to face all of these problems.

One of the most important services has been the promotion of health. This ministry began as a service to the really ill. We discovered that families hid lepers, the mentally ill, cancer patients in the last stages, in dark corners of their houses or backyards.

Our first ministers of health visited the homes and united the families with their ill members to pray together and to integrate the ill into the daily lives of the whole family. These ministers, however, discovered that there were many other diseases that the children or elderly had that could be avoided by good hygiene or preventive medicine.

Also, for the poor, there are many herbs in Brazil that can be used as medicines. They can be grown in backyards or picked in fields. Our ministers still visit homes, but they also give courses in preventive medicine and teach the families how to care for their sick members.

São Paulo is one of the urban centres that has an immense number of people suffering from AIDS, or HIV-positive. Years ago the problem was infected blood in transfusions and homosexual activity. Today we also have those infected when they share the same needle for drugs. More and more women are being infected by their companions or while taking drugs. The majority of women who die between twenty and thirty years of age die from AIDS. Sadder still is the large number of babies that are born HIV-positive.

We have many programmes in São Paulo to serve these people. Our ministers visit them in their homes and teach their families how to care for them and how to help them die without despair. One of their most important tasks is to help them overcome the conviction that AIDS is a divine punishment! We have opened houses all over the city for people who have no families or who are rejected by their families. We have several houses for the infected babies. It is sad to see that in many neighbourhoods, the families who live near to these houses are terrified of being infected by the babies! We still have much to do to help our religious people to learn to love and live the way of peace.

One of our most serious problems in São Paulo is the women, almost all of them with children, who are widows or abandoned by their companions. Over 40% of the families in São Paulo are one-parent families, and this means that the one parent is a woman. Some of these women become prostitutes because they can find no other way to support their children.

Others collect and sell paper and bottles, returning home exhausted and broken. The children are left alone all day. One of our most heartbreaking services has been to these women and their children. They are now organized, and have even national meetings to discuss their problems and overcome their difficulties.

The different services I have mentioned here, and many others that I have not the time to mention, are for us the way to true peace. As I have said at the beginning, inner peace and peaceful relations are not the natural condition of the human being. We have to learn to build a society in peace so that we can live in a peaceful world.

There will never be peace in Latin America, in Japan, or in the world if we do not build step by step, day by day, the conditions for peace. The way of peace is the object of our faith. It is the meaning of our lives in this suffering world.

Religion and Human Rights

DESMOND TUTU

*The author is Anglican Archbishop of Capetown; he has
been awarded the Nobel Peace Prize*

In a country like South Africa, which for decades was
characterized by racial tensions and conflicts, a Declaration on
a Global Ethic supported by people with a religious commitment whose skins are of many colours is particularly important. In our struggle for democracy and justice, we have
experienced how important it is for people to act in accordance with ethical norms and moral convictions, especially in
the sphere of politics. It makes a great difference whether
politics is done in accordance with irrevocable commitments
of the kind endorsed by the Parliament's Declaration: commitment to a culture of non-violence and respect for life;
commitment to a culture of solidarity and a just economic
order; commitment to a culture of tolerance and a life of
truthfulness; commitment to a culture of equal rights and
partnership between men and women. So I support this
Declaration with all my heart; it represents important progress
in the history of the world's religions. The text which follows is
not a direct commentary on this Declaration; it was originally
written as a lecture which I gave at Emory University, Atlanta,
in October 1994. However, the attentive reader will note that
at the end of it I already refer to the Declaration, and that my
basic approach on the question of religion and human rights is
identical with the principles laid down in the Declaration.

Every human being is an image of God

Here is quite a well known story. When the missionaries came to Africa, they had the Bible and we, the natives, had the land. They said 'Let us pray', and we dutifully shut our eyes. When we opened them, they had the land and we had the Bible. On the surface, it would appear that we had struck a bad bargain. However, the fact of the matter is that we came out of that transaction a great deal better off than when we started. The point is that we were given a priceless gift in the word of God, the gospel of salvation, the good news of God's utterly unconditional love for us. But even more wonderful is the fact that we were given the most subversive, most revolutionary thing around. Those who may have wanted to exploit us and to subject us to injustice and oppression should really not have given us the Bible because that placed dynamite under their nefarious schemes.

The Bible makes some quite staggering assertions about human beings which came to be the foundations of the culture of basic human rights that have become so commonplace in our day and age. Both creation narratives in Genesis 1–3 assert quite categorically that human beings are the pinnacle, the climax, of the divine creative activity; if not climactic, then central or crucial to the creative activity. In the first narrative the whole creative process moves impressively to its climax, which is the creation of human beings. The author signals that something quite out of the ordinary is about to happen by a change in the formula relating to a creative divine action. Up to this point God has merely had to say 'Let there be . . . ' and by the divine *fiat* something springs into being *ex nihilo*. At this climactic point God first invites his heavenly court to participate with him, 'Let us create man in our image' – something special has come into being.

This is remarkable in a piece that is in fact in part intended to be jingoistic propaganda, designed to lift the sagging spirits of a people in exile whose fortunes are at a low ebb, surrounded as they are by the impressive monuments to Babylonian hegemony. Where one would have expected the author to claim that only Jews were created in the image of God, this passage asserts that all human beings have been created in the divine image.

That this attribute is a universal phenomenon was not necessarily self-evident. Someone as smart as Aristotle taught that human personality was not universally possessed by all human beings, because slaves in his view were not persons. The biblical teaching is marvellously exhilarating in a situation of oppression and injustice, because in that situation it has often been claimed that certain groups were inferior or superior because they had or did not have a particular attribute (physical or cultural). The Bible claims for all human beings this exalted status that we are all, each one of us, created in the divine image. This has nothing to do with this or that extraneous attribute which by the nature of the case can be possessed by only some people.

The consequences that flow from these biblical assertions are quite staggering. First, human life (as all life) is a gift from the gracious and ever-generous Creator of all. It is therefore inviolable. We must therefore have a deep reverence for the sanctity of human life. That is why homicide is universally condemned. 'Thou shalt not kill' would be an undisputed part of a global ethic accepted by the adherents of all faiths and of none. For many it would include as an obvious corollary the prohibition of capital punishment. It has seemed an oddity that we should want to demonstrate our outrage that, for example, someone had shown scant reverence for human life by committing murder, by ourselves then proceeding to take another life. In some ways this is an irrational obscenity.

The life of every human person is inviolable as a gift from God. And since this person is created in the image of God and is a God-carrier, a second consequence would be that we should not just respect such a person, but that we should have a deep reverence for that person. The New Testament claims that the Christian person becomes a sanctuary, a temple of the Holy Spirit, someone who is indwelt by the most holy and blessed Trinity. We would want to assert this of all human beings. We should not just greet one another. We should strictly genuflect before such an august and precious creature. The Buddhist is correct in bowing profoundly before another human being, as the God in me acknowledges and greets the God in you.

This preciousness, this infinite worth, is intrinsic to all we are, and is inalienable as a gift from God, to be acknowledged as an inalienable right of all human persons.

The Babylonian creation narrative makes human beings have a low destiny and purpose – as those intended to be the scavengers of the gods. Not so the biblical world-view, which declares that the human being created in the image of God is meant to be God's viceroy, God's representative in having rule over the rest of creation on behalf of God. To have dominion, not in an authoritarian and destructive manner, but to hold sway as God would hold sway – compassionately, gently, caringly; enabling each part of creation to come fully into its own and to realize its potential for the good of the whole, contributing to the harmony and unity which was God's intention for the whole of creation. And even more wonderfully, this human person is destined to know and to love God, and to dwell with the divine for ever and ever, enjoying unspeakable celestial delights. Nearly all major religions envisage a *post mortem* existence for humankind that far surpasses anything we can conceive.

All this makes human beings unique. It imbues each one of us with profound dignity and worth. So to treat people as if they were less than this, to oppress them, to trample their dignity underfoot, is not just evil, as it surely must be; it is not just painful, as it frequently must be, for the victims of injustice and oppression. It is positively blasphemous, for it is tantamount to spitting in the face of God. That is why we have been so passionate in our opposition to the evil of apartheid. We have not, as some might mischievously have supposed, been driven by political or ideological considerations. No, we have been constrained by the imperatives of our biblical faith.

Any person of faith has no real option. In the face of injustice and oppression it is disobedience to God not to stand up in opposition to that injustice and that oppression. Any violation of the rights of God's stand-in cries out to be condemned and to be redressed, and all people of good will must willy-nilly be engaged in upholding and preserving those rights as a religious duty. Such a discussion as this should therefore not be merely an academic exercise in the most pejorative sense. It must be able to galvanize participants with a zeal to be active protectors of the rights of persons.

Human freedom and liberation

The Bible points to the fact that human persons are endowed with freedom to choose. This freedom is constitutive of what it means to be a person – one who has the freedom to choose between alternative options, and to choose freely (apart from the influences of heredity and nurture). To be a person is to be able to choose to love or not to love, to be able to reject or to accept the offer of the divine love, to be free to obey or to disobey. That is what constitutes being a moral agent.

We cannot properly praise or blame someone who does what he/she cannot help doing, or refrains from doing what he/she cannot help not doing. Moral approbation and disapproval have no meaning where there is no freedom to choose between various options on offer. That is what enables us to have moral responsibility. An automaton cannot be a moral agent, and therein lies our glory and our damnation. We may choose aright, and therein is bliss; or we may choose wrongly, and therein lies perdition. God may not intervene to nullify this incredible gift in order to stop us from making wrong choices. I have said on other occasions that God, who alone has the perfect right to be a totalitarian, has such a profound reverence for our freedom that he had much rather we went freely to hell than compel us to go to heaven.

An unfree human being is a contradiction in terms. To be

human is to be free. God gives us space to be free and so to be human. Human beings have an autonomy, an integrity, which should not be violated, which should not be subverted. St Paul exults as he speaks of what he calls the 'glorious liberty of the children of God', and elsewhere declares that Christ has set us free for freedom.

It is a freedom to hold any view or none – freedom of expression. It is freedom of association because we are created for family, for togetherness, for community, because the solitary human being is an aberration.

We are created to exist in a delicate network of interdependence with fellow human beings and the rest of God's creation. All sorts of things go horribly badly wrong when we break this fundamental law of our being. Then we are no longer appalled as we should be that vast sums are spent on budgets of death and destruction, when a tiny fraction of those sums would ensure that God's children everywhere would have a clean supply of water, adequate health care, proper housing and education, enough to eat and to wear. A totally self-sufficient human being would be subhuman.

Perhaps because of their own experience of slavery, the Israelites depicted God as the great liberator, and they seemed to be almost obsessed with being set free. So they had the principle of Jubilee enshrined in the heart of the biblical tradition. It was unnatural for anyone to be enthralled to another, and so every seven years and every seventy years they celebrated Jubilee, when those who had become slaves were set at liberty. Those who had mortgaged their land received it back unencumbered by the burden of debt, reminding everyone that all they were and all they had was gift; that absolute ownership belonged to God; that all were really equal before God, who was the real and true Sovereign.

The positive influence of religion

That is the basis of the egalitarianism of the Bible – that all belongs to God and that all are of equal worth in God's sight. That is heady stuff. No political ideology could better that for radicalness. And that is what fired our own struggle against apartheid – this incredible sense of the infinite worth of each person created in the image of God, being God's viceroy, God's representative, God's stand-in, being a God-carrier, a sanctuary, a temple of the Holy Spirit; inviolate, possessing a dignity that was intrinsic with an autonomy and freedom to choose that were constitutive of human personality.

This person was meant to be creative, to resemble God in his creativity. So wholesome work is something humans need to be truly human. The biblical understanding of being human includes freedom from fear and insecurity, freedom from penury and want, freedom of association and movement because we would live ideally in the kind of society that is characterized by these attributes. It would be a caring and compassionate, a sharing and gentle society in which, like God, the strongest would be concerned about the welfare of the weakest – represented in ancient society by the widow, the alien and the orphan; in which you reflected the holiness of God not by ritual, purity and cultic correctness but by the fact that when you gleaned your harvest, you left something behind for the poor, the unemployed, the marginalized ones – all a declaration of the unique worth of persons that does not hinge on the economic, social or political status but simply on the fact that they are persons created in God's image. That is what invests them with their preciousness and from this stem all kinds of rights.

All the above is the positive impact that religion can have as well as the consequences that flow from these fundamental assertions. Sadly, and often tragically, religion is not often in and of itself necessarily a good thing. Already in the Bible there is ample evidence that religion can be a baneful thing, often with horrendous consequences for its adherents or those who may be designated its unfortunate targets. Frequent strictures are levelled at religious observance which is just a matter of external form, when the obsession is with cultic minutiae and correctness. Such religion is considered to be an abomination, however elaborate the ritual performed. Its worth is tested by whether it has any significant impact on how its adherents treat especially the widow, the orphan and the alien in the midst. How one deals with those who have no real clout and who can make no claim on being given equitable and compassionate treatment becomes a vital clue to the quality of religiosity.

This certainly says many things, one of which is surely that God recognizes a particular worth in those who, humanly speaking, are non-entities. It is a paradox that God should show his graciousness, mercy and love through his concern through those whom the world considers to be so utterly lacking in social, political or economic significance, and it must be that they do have a worth that does not depend on these extrinsic attributes.

There have been some glorious moments inspired by the religious faiths in which people believe. Frequently in our struggle against the evil that was apartheid, we stood arm in arm as Christians with Jews, Muslims and Hindus. And what a glorious vindication happened with the inauguration of Nelson Mandela as the first democratically elected President of a liberated, a new South Africa! Many acknowledge the crucial role that religious leaders played to bring to birth the new and free South Africa.

Pathological aspects of religion

We must hang our heads in shame when we survey the gory and shameful history of the church of Christ. Umpteen wars of religion have been instigated by those who claimed to be followers of the One described as the Prince of Peace. The Crusades, using the cross as a distinctive emblem, were waged in order to commend the Good News of this Prince of Peace amongst the infidel Muslims, seeking to ram down people's throats a faith that somewhere thought it prided itself on the autonomy of the individual person freely to choose to believe or not to believe. Religious zealots have seemed blind to the incongruity and indeed contradiction of using constraint of whatever sort to proclaim a religion that sets high store by individual freedom of choice. Several bloody conflicts characterize the history of Christianity, and war is without doubt the most comprehensive violation of human rights. It ignores reverence for life in its wanton destruction of people. It subverts social and family life and justifies the abrogation of fundamental rights.

Christians have waged wars against fellow-Christians. Saint Paul was flabbergasted that Christians could bring charges against fellow-Christians in a court of law. It is not difficult to imagine what he would have felt and what he would have said about the spectacle of Christians liquidating fellow-Christians as in war. Christians have been grossly intolerant of one another, as when Christians persecuted fellow-Christians for holding different views about religious dogma and practice. The Inquisition and all that is associated with it is a considerable blot on our copybook. The church has had fewer more inglorious occasions than those when the Inquisition was active. Christians have gone on an orgy of excommunicating one another just because of disagreements about doctrine, etc; not to mention the downright obscurantism displayed in the persecution of the likes of Galileo and Copernicus for propounding intellectual views that were anathema to the church at the time.

Slavery is an abominable affront to the dignity of those who would be treated as if they were mere chattels. The trade in fellow human beings should have been recognized as completely contrary to the central tenets of Christianity about the unspeakable worth and preciousness of each human person. And yet Christians were some of the most zealous slave owners, who opposed the efforts of emancipators such as William Wilberforce. The Civil War in the USA in part happened because of differences of opinion on the vexed question of slavery. Devout Christians saw no inconsistency between singing Christian hymns lustily and engaging in this demeaning trade in fellow humans. Indeed, one of the leading hymn-writers of the day was also an enthusiastic slave owner. Christians have been foremost supporters of antisemitism, blaming Jews for committing deicide in crucifying Jesus Christ.

A devastating chapter in human history happened with Hitler's final solution, culminating in the Holocaust. Hitler purported to be a Christian, and saw no contradiction between his Christianity and perpetrating one of history's most dastardly campaigns. What is even more disturbing is that he was supported in this massive crime against humanity by a significant group called German Christians. Mercifully there were those like Dietrich Bonhoeffer and others who opposed this madness, often at great cost to themselves as members of the Confessing Church. Christianity has often been perversely used in other instances to justify the iniquity of racism. In the USA, the rabid haters of blacks, the Ku Klux Klan, have not balked at using a flaming cross as their much-feared symbol. One would have to travel far to find a more despicable example of blasphemy. Apartheid in South Africa was perpetrated not by pagans but by those who regarded themselves as devout Christians. Their opponents, even though known to be Christians, were usually vilified as Communists and worse. Many conflicts in the world have been started and certainly been made worse by religious and sectarian differences: the conflicts in Northern Ireland and in the Sudan; many of the conflicts in the Indian sub-continent and in the Middle East. Religious differences have exacerbated the horrendous blood-letting in Bosnia euphemistically described as ethnic cleansing.

Religion, which should produce peace, reconciliation, tolerance and respect for human rights, has often promoted the opposite conditions. And yet the potential for great good in the impact and influence of religion remains, and was recognized by the Parliament of the World's Religions meeting last year in Chicago, which produced a call for a global ethic. There would be no new global order unless there was first a global ethic which would be 'a fundamental consensus concerning binding values, irrevocable standards and personal attitudes'.

I can testify that our own struggle for justice, peace and equity would have floundered badly had we not been inspired by our Christian faith and assured of the ultimate victory of goodness and truth, compassion and love, against their ghastly counterparts. We want to promote freedom of religion as an indispensable part of any genuinely free society.

From the World of Islam

Towards a New Way of Thinking

CROWN PRINCE HASSAN BIN TALAL

The author is Crown Prince of the Hashemite Kingdom of Jordan and one of the great promoters of understanding between the religions

The Declaration of the Parliament of the World's Religions embodies the highest aspirations of humanity. I believe that it points the way towards a new thinking for the twenty-first century and beyond.

The great challenges for humankind

Since the Industrial Revolution, we have tried to harness forces whose consequences we have only recently begun to comprehend. The domestication of plants and animals represented an equally giant step ten thousand years ago; but the consequences of the Agricultural Revolution were played out over millennia, and went hand in hand with gradual change in the patterns of human life and thought. The radical transformations wrought by industrialization have swept the world in a matter of two centuries. They have not as yet been accompanied by an appropriate shift in human consciousness. The outcome has been a brush with ecological disaster unparalleled in our history. At the same time, humanity's eternal war against itself has been stoked by the invention of ever more effective implements of destruction.

With the onset of the Information Revolution in our time, and the concomitant quickening of the global pulse, we face perhaps the greatest challenges that our species has yet confronted. At this time, when our needs would seem to be overwhelmingly practical, of what use are our spiritual traditions and our ethical beliefs?

If we are to survive these changes, we must evolve a new thinking. Such a thinking must be able to see the inter-connections and inter-dependence between peoples, cultures and religions, while respecting their diversity. It must develop the vision to identify and build upon common fundamentals. It should not ask us to abandon our cultural baggage, but merely to recognize it for what it is. Only when we have developed such a thinking will we be able to live in peace with each other, and in peace with our world. If this new way is to succeed, it must be grounded in our common past, and within the bounds of human experience. We must re-discover and promote anew the notions of balance, tolerance and empathy. We must find again the ability to listen with respect to the voices of others, to see the whole as well as the parts, to extend participation to all. And it is here that our spiritual traditions play their part.

Ecologists agree that a global balance needs to be struck between human, environmental and economic considerations. Such a balance should acknowledge that certain aims, such as the elimination of poverty, the provision of energy and fresh water for all, and the reduction of conflict on all levels, are not negotiable. Changes in current patterns of production must be made by the industrialized nations. Support for developing countries, the transfer of environmentally sensitive technology, and aid through trade, all represent central components of such a global balance. It is not possible to ignore the connections between different regions of the world. It is, rather, imperative that all find the common ground necessary to work together.

All human beings are dependent on one another

New visions are therefore our most vital and precious strategic resource. The rapid economic development model, with its environmental strains and human alienation, must give way to a new paradigm, sensitive both to the needs of the environment and the welfare of people. The articulation of such a model, harmonizing the needs of the environment with the demands of development, is among the key imperatives of our time.

This is an age of mass communications, rapid industrialization, instant decision-making; an age in which our earth and all it contains are subject to inconceivable pressures. Now more than ever, it is imperative to appreciate in advance the consequences of our actions. The changes sweeping the world mean that there can be no room for insularity. There is room only for those who acknowledge our mutual inter-dependence, and who strive to enrich our common lot. The search for peace starts here.

It is often said that the foundation of peace is justice; but what is justice? It has been defined as 'treating like cases alike; and different cases differently'. The key to justice lies in our definitions of 'like' and 'different'. Injustice is perceived, and conflict results, when the gap between 'self' and 'other', between 'me' and 'thee', seems to be larger than the common ground. Conflict most often occurs when a fundamental and threatening difference is perceived. The split between subject and object is thus at the root of all oppositions, all polarities, all conflicts. Peace, then, is a dynamic state of mutual interconnection in which notions of 'self' and 'other' are sufficiently broad that individuals are able to identify and empathize with one another across the divides created by culture and ideology.

The Declaration towards a Global Ethic agreed upon by the Parliament of the World's Religions represents a substantive attempt to bridge those divides. By providing a starting point that all can agree upon, a Global Ethic would begin to traverse the split between subject and object. It would identify the fundamentals that are common to all religious traditions, and distill from them the essence of human belief.

A global ethic should constitute a core of belief, acceptable to all. It should not seek to impose one vision, or to legislate away our differences. It should strive for unity, but seek neither to eradicate nor to compromise diversity. After all, in this global age, only a truly global ethic can be of real value.

That this has been the approach of the Parliament is cause for great optimism. I congratulate all those involved in the drafting of the Declaration, for their work paves the way for all our futures.

Striving for a Higher Ethic

MUHAMMAD EL-GHAZALI

The author is a sheikh at the Al-Azhar University in Cairo

I felt a sense of satisfaction as I read about the establishment of an international organization to reinforce and promote higher ethics among mankind. It confirmed my belief that the nature of humanity is basically good, kind, loving, seeking perfection and resisting the 'money-madness' that confines man to his own selfish ends.

Readiness for peace – and a proviso

The nations of the world are now closely linked together despite geographical remoteness, and for the first time in world history there is an international organization comprising all nations of the world. The whole universe is now a small village that can come closer, negotiate and study rising problems, and work towards their solution.

However, such higher objectives can only be attained in the light of superior ethics and morals, and suppression of egoism and prejudice. The question is: will we fail to provide the means required to reach our aspirations and objectives?

The Prophet of Islam says: 'I have been sent for the completion and perfection of the nobler ethics.' The Prophet once said to his nephew Ali Bin Abi Taleb: 'Do you wish to know the ultimate and most refined in ethics for both life and the afterlife? It is to maintain kinship ties even with those who have shunned you, to give to those who have deprived you, and to forgive those who have wronged you.' He further added to his friends, 'Shall I tell you of an even better and superior status than that achieved through fasting, prayer and almsgiving? Reconcile your enmities, for enmity and hostility disfigure the faith.'

As Muslims we are happy that such an organization for global ethics has been formed to support and aid the UN in objective decision-making.

Frankly, however, I felt a sense of uneasiness when I learnt that the Parliament of the World's Religions has opened its door for the participation of both believers and non-believers, monotheists and polytheists, those who believe in the immortality of the spirit and those who believe in the termination of existence upon death.

But then it may be argued that the world comprises people of diverse religions and beliefs and that the UN consists of nations of conflicting religious sects who sit side by side to study and discuss various issues and problems. Consequently, a global ethics organization can do no less.

My comment on such a claim would be the following. To consider the belief in God as a secondary, side issue, or an issue that is altogether unrelated to ethics, is something that is objectionable to us Muslims. In fact, it raises feelings of aversion and revolt. Why should God be the Creator and others be worshipped in His stead? Why should God be the Giver and Provider and others be thanked instead? Why should ingratitude be considered a vice except in our relationship with God?

If one is generous and giving to others and is reciprocated with total ingratitude, this would create ill feelings and resentment within him. How can one concede to the presence of those who continually benefit from God's endowments and then dare to deny His existence and consequently their obligations towards Him?

The moral power of religion

I think that atheists should be disregarded in this respect, but if we have to sit with them, then a special policy must be laid down to harmonize between our religious faith and their rights in life. Who knows, maybe our congeniality will one day guide them to the right and true path.

As Muslims, it gives us great pleasure to meet with followers of the heavenly religions that preceded Islam in a global conference where goodness is highly esteemed and folly is condemned; where we can promote virtue and combat vice.

There is much more to be said in this regard. The heritage the Prophet Mohammed left us lacks nothing in terms of a complete ethical guide about how to perfect morality and rise above pettiness and selfishness. It is an enormous heritage, that consists of hundreds of pages filled with elaborations on noble ethics.

I do not know of another heaven-sent Prophet or worldly philosopher who has left such a heritage. As Muslims, we like to become acquainted with others, and likewise, for people to get to know us. For thus God has taught us: He did not create the earth for us to live in constant dispute and bloodshed. To the contrary, He created the earth so that we may utilize His endowments and duly thank Him for them: 'God is the One who made the Earth docile to you. So walk upon its shoulders, eat of His sustenance. Unto Him will be the Resurrection' (Surah 67. 15).

It is sad that Jews and Christians do not reciprocate the same kind of treatment with Muslims. In fact, I once read that a Jew in the city of Al-Khalil seized the house of an Arab and told the owner: 'This was my house several thousands of years ago and now it has returned to my ownership. I will not ask you for its rent for the past centuries, but I will ask you to go live elsewhere – or out in the open if you so wish – but never come back here . . . or else . . . !' How can any form of human relationship be properly established based on this kind of logic?

This was the same kind of rationale underlying imperialist policies throughout past eras. Islam was accused by some of having conquered the Roman Empire which ruled Anatolia, the Eastern Mediterranean, the Nile Valley, North Africa and many other lands. Islam ousted the Romans and returned those regions to their native rulers, who voluntarily converted to Islam. The Roman ancestors now look upon the old colonies as their long-lost property that must be retrieved, and look upon the millions of Muslims as their ancient slaves.

No doubt the establishment of the UN on purely humanitarian grounds has opened a new page in world history and reduced feelings of hostility of past imperialism – but have the victors who founded this honourable organization rid themselves of the old resentment and banished all bigotry and greed? The establishment of a global ethics organization may support higher humanitarian values and characteristics, and activate and enhance efforts towards their promotion, thereby aiding the UN to attain its objectives and prevent the hazards of division and dispute in the world.

The commandment of justice

In a divine hadith, God revealed to his Prophet: 'O worshippers, I have prohibited injustice unto myself as I have prohibited it amongst you; so do not commit injustice.' And in another divine hadith, He says: 'Beware and guard against being unjust, for injustice shall cover you in darkness on the Day of Reckoning.'

We believe that men of faith are honourable and dignified in contentment and in anger – they do not transgress upon others' rights, nor do they persecute the weak. They are content with justice and righteousness – for ruthlessness and transgression are the characteristics of beasts rather than humans.

It is sad that throughout its history, humanity has connived to commit injustices and seen in the diversity of mankind – strong v. weak, wealthy v. poor, believers v. non-believers – a loophole through which it has committed acts of transgression.

The Qur'an clearly opposes the interference of anything moral or physical with the process of justice: 'O you who believe, stand up firmly for justice as witnesses for God, even as against yourselves, or your parents, or your near of kin, whether it be against rich or poor, God can best protect them. So follow not your lusts, lest you deviate, for if you twist or turn, then surely God is All-Aware of what you do' (4.135). In another verse He says: 'And let not detestation of a people move you to be unfair; be equitable, that is closer to piety; and fear God. God is well aware of all that you do' (5.8).

People believed that religious differences sanctioned injustice, thus leading to deviant emotions and reckless whims and desires. This is entirely untrue, for God has sent His messenger with a totally different message: 'And God enjoins justice, and good deeds and generosity' (16.90).

I will cite here three of the Prophet's hadiths that refute these allegations against Islam:

1. 'The prayer of the oppressed is answered in Heaven without fail, his immorality notwithstanding.'

2. 'The prayer of the oppressed, even the non-believer, is quick to reach Heaven' (is promptly answered by God).

3. When the Prophet was asked about the scriptures of Abraham he answered: 'They were in the form of sayings such as: "O, thou imposing, afflicted and vain king, I have not sent thee to gather worldly wealth but to answer the prayers of the oppressed and restore justice on my behalf – for I do not shun such a prayer even coming from a non-believer."'

It is noteworthy that when the Prophet of Islam died, his shield was still mortgaged with a Jew for food he had bought. (Religious differences did not affect relations in this case.) A Jew lived peaceably in the capital of Islam, not fearing for his safety, his family or his money. Certainly his estrangement did not result in his oppression. Islamic rule protected the Jew's rights, so that he lived and died without cause for grievance.

As Muslims, we respect all views and counter-views, but our own grievance is the long-standing heritage of malevolence with which Muslims are treated in various spheres of life. This, we trust, will ultimately disappear with the establishment of human rights.

The Religions Must Work Together

HASSAN HANAFI

The author is Professor of Philosophy in the University of Cairo

The Declaration of the Parliament of the World's Religions reveals the possibility of the convergence of all religions towards a global ethic. Morality is the common basis of all religions. Religions diverge in ways of understanding and implementing this morality in perception (images), in action (rituals), in principle (dogmas) and in institutions (establishments). The simplicity of the Declaration comes from the simplicity of primitive life and the evidence of morality. A human consensus in religion would help in minimizing the dangers of particularism in the present era.

However, it is difficult to put aside the theological and philosophical foundations of a global ethic. Incarnation, resurrection, redemption, etc. are symbols of morality. *Tawhid* in Islam is the basis of the Islamic universal code of ethics. In fact, the Declaration is based on Kantian normative ethics, on 'should', not on 'is'. A combination of idealism and realism, of normativeness and pragmaticism (not pragmatism), as in Schiller, would also be desirable. There can be no Declaration on a Global Ethic without an implied philosophy.

Problems of practical application

The Declaration is written as a human discourse which satisfies the masses and the elites, the common man and the expert. However, the 'Introduction', which is a summary of the Declaration, is somewhat rhetorical. Some statistical data and quantitative analyses of pollution, poverty, violence, etc., would link the discourse to reality and prevent some repetitions.

The transformation of the normative discourse expressed by 'should' into a realistic discourse expressed by 'is' would be very beneficial. The norm cannot be implemented except in fact. The imperative of the subject will stay void unless it is realized in an object. The vision of the Torah, the style of the Ten Commandments, can be linked to the analysis of universal intentions of revelation (in Islam): the preservation of life, of reason, of truth, of honour and of human wealth and natural resources. A formal categorical imperative can intertwine with a material value ethic. A transformation of consciousness is parallel to a change in the human condition.

It may be true that the Declaration is too Western, given the concentration on ecology, not on development; on human rights more than on people's rights; on individual ethics more than on social groups; on ethics more than on politics; on the inside more than on the outside. In Asia, Africa and Latin America the major challenges come from the real world, not from the good will; from social structure, not from individual moral consciousness.

Generalities, principles and a declaration of intent are not enough to tackle the actual problems which prevent the religious dialogue, such as oppression, exploitation, domination, acculturation, dependence and so on. It is also important to know how this global ethic can be implemented, combining the 'how' with the 'what', adding instrumental reason to legitimizing reason. The analysis of material and efficient causes is no less important than the description of formal and even of final causes. No new global order without a new global ethic. No new global ethic without a new socio-political reality.

The problem of minorities in the Islamic world

New categories, more neutral, have to be used for a more
balanced vision as long as the dichotomy between the centre
and the periphery prevails. The problem of minorities in the
Muslim world is not an ethnic problem but a result of the
absence of political, social and cultural pluralism. The problem of women is indeed a manifestation of another primary
problem, that of citizenship, including men and women. This
calls for commitment to a culture of equal rights and
partnership between men and women without forgetting the
citizenship to which men and women belong.

The practice of violence by dissident individuals and groups
is a reaction to another form of violence practised by states.
The first may be a liberating violence, while the second is an
oppressive violence. There is a need for commitment to a
culture of non-violence and respect for life and to get rid of the
spiral of violence of great powers and oppressive regimes,
generating the liberating violence of small states and individ-
uals/groups.

Bahai'ism is after all an Islamic sect within Shi'ism, just as
Anglicanism is a Christian sect under Protestantism or any
mystical order under Catholicism. Baha'i is is not an indepen-
dent religion. A variation of Shi'ism such as Ismailism,
Qadanism, and so on cannot be an independent religion if
Shi'ism itself is a part of Islam.

Muslim representation in the Declaration is weak. Muslim
representatives are mostly individuals or some institutions not
from the heartland of Islam. A more diversified and heavy
representation from religious leaders, intellectuals, core institutions, is desirable.

Islamic input into the formulation of the Declaration is also
weak. In Islamic jurisprudence, theoretical truth is multiple,
while practical truth is one. Many religions with different
world-views and belief-systems can co-operate in realizing one
common blueprint for human survival and the common
welfare of mankind. All those who share a universal code of

ethics and implement it in the good deed belong to the same human fundamental consensus. Jews, Christians, Brahmans, Confucianists, Sabeans, Mages, etc. share in the same code and practise the same virtue.

Unresolved questions of world politics and world justice

The question the Muslims are asking is why Islam is taken as a substitute enemy after the collapse of Communism. Why is the West antagonizing Islam by abandoning the Bosnians, the Chechens, etc. to the most horrible genocide since the Holocaust? Why is the West supporting the dictatorial regimes in the Muslim world against the will of the people expressed by Islamic movements, including fundamentalist ones?

The Arab-Israeli conflict is not a conflict between Jews and Muslims. Both Judaism and Islam belong to the same root, the religion of Abraham. Judaism and Christianity are integral parts of Islam. It is an Arab-Israeli conflict in so far as the Golan Heights and Southern Lebanon are occupied, and a Palestinian-Israeli dispute in so far as the West Bank including Jerusalem is still occupied. It is a political problem with religious justification, not a religious dispute. There is a need for commitment to a culture of tolerance and a life of truthfulness once justice is done for all people, not the solving of one problem, the Jewish Diaspora, in such a way as to create another problem, the Palestinian Diaspora.

A redistribution of world wealth over the world population has to be stressed. Up to now, 5% of the world population is consuming 30% of world commodities. Millions in Africa, Asia and Latin America are dying from drought, hunger and disease. There is a need for commitment to a culture of solidarity and a just economic order after changing the actual maldistribution of world wealth over people of the world for a juster distribution between the centre and the periphery. The wealth in the centre accumulated during European modern times has to return back to the periphery. Decolonization occurred on the political level, but it has not yet occurred on the economic and cultural levels.

World history has to be rewritten in a more just way in order to put European modern times, less than five hundred years, in a longer view of world history lasting millennia, in China, India, Mesopotamia, Persia, Egypt, etc. Justice has to be re-established in historiography, the major source of people's images and counter-images and for implementing peace in the world. The historical super-value of the centre has to return back to the periphery. In fact, the Declaration tries to go beyond Eurocentrism. Humanity is much larger than Western humanity. The Universal Declarations on Human Rights, on People's Rights, on a Global Ethic, are not confined to European borders. In the Third World, there are still some suspicions about terms like universal, global and human, applied to the centre alone or including the periphery. A fundamental demand is: every human being must be treated humanely, not in a way confined to the geographical borders of Europe, nor with a double standard depending on the situation, whether inside or outside Europe.

On Human Unity and Equality

MAHMOUD ZAKZOUK

The author is Dean of the Faculty of Islamic Theology in the Al-Azhar University, Cairo

The world-wide human ethic which, as the Declaration of the Parliament of the World's Religions emphasizes, can rescue humankind from destruction, is also the ethic, binding on all human beings, which stands at the centre of Islamic teaching.

Man as God's governor

In many parts of the world we have now become aware that individuals, and also individual communities, can achieve moral perfection only if they allow themselves to be guided not by the material but by the transcendent.

This happens in accordance with the plan of creation if human beings use their freedom to raise themselves above their one-sidedly materialistic and egotistic wishes by following ethical commands. In so doing they fulfil their human destiny as God's governor in this world. All humans originally come from one being (Surah 4. 1). The numerous differences which exist between them should not be a reason for senseless power struggles, but the necessary stimulus to human development, to effort at mutual respect, a reasonable understanding and a collaboration which is fruitful precisely because of its difficulties (Surah 49. 13). Since in terms of their origin, despite all their differences, human beings form a unity, one injures the whole of humankind if one injures one person; and conversely, if one does good to one person, one helps all humankind (Surah 5.32).

The Qur'an teaches that since the creation of human beings it has been revealed to them through the prophets how they can find their destiny and the happiness they desire without unnecessary and self-destructive deviations: they will do so if they follow the guidelines of the revelations consistently. For they are destined to a life in dignity, to a life of joy in creation, and not to be lost by fighting against one another and destroying one another in a senseless way.

Acting with responsible awareness

The precondition for this is that they maintain the order of creation and occupy the leading place in it to which they are destined. This again is possible only if they act with responsible awareness – each in his own environment – and do not allow themselves to be driven indiscriminately. They can do that if they believe and act rightly, i.e. surrender themselves to the guidance of the Transcendent.

For they are only apparently separate individuals. As the Prophet Muhammad once described it, they are all in a ship which will sink unless they recognize their responsibility for their actions, for themselves, for their fellow human beings and the whole of creation, and are concerned to behave reasonably in accordance with this.

'Wish for other people what you wish for yourself, and you will become a Muslim,' the Prophet Muhammad once said. The deepest human wishes for happiness, harmony and peace will be fulfilled by brotherliness and a love of justice and peace. But the only way to this is through the human action of acknowledging the other person in principle as oneself.

Collaboration and understanding are possible because of the fundamental equality of all human beings and the bond between them. But the individual and the community realize this equality and bond only when they dare to hope for the help of the transcendent and devote themselves to the fulfilment of the ethic which is enjoined on all human beings.

Whenever something good is done to a person, something good is done to the whole of humankind. And the spiritual treasures of wisdom and religion which have been handed down to all humankind teach us that one can do the good if one is seriously concerned to do so. In that case one will become a model on which other people, indeed even the whole of humankind, can orientate themselves. So specifically as a Muslim I would like to express my support for the Declaration on a Global Ethic and wish it success with all my heart.

A Charter of Duties and Tasks for All Human Beings

MUHAMMAD TALBI

The author is Professor of Islamic History at the University of Tunis

The religions used to be the only purveyors of ethics. All in all they were the supreme criterion of trustworthiness. With the advent of modernity, which was synonymous with emancipation, their throne has been more or less severely shaken. To different degrees, they have lost much of their power, and everywhere, as a global system and structure, they have constantly given ground to secularization, whether officially and sometimes quite aggressively proclaimed, or more or less discreet and unacknowledged. They still have heaven in cases of doubt, but on earth Caesar does not cease to call the tune. All the nostalgia for the past, all attempts to row desperately against the current, are useless in the long term. The religions have definitively lost the monopoly of ethics.

Religion as a foundation for values

It seems clear and almost indisputable that today the world has reached a level of development at which it needs a planetary, global ethic. About fifteen years ago I wrote: 'Historians cannot fail to note that we have left the era of civilizations. Perhaps we have not yet reached the era of Civilization, but we have already turned the corner and passed the point of no return. In future there will only be civilizations which can be isolated by historical analysis and confined within the limits of an epithet which defines their geographical or ethnic contours. In the past, even outside influences contributed towards modelling and reinforcing specific internal characteristics. Today the barriers are falling. In the future which is opening up before our eyes the permeability which is coming about at every level as a result of mass communication, the melting down, the levelling out, will spread to an unprecedented degree. Communication will continue to diversify and gain influence; it is far from having said its last word. These factors will act irresistibly, whether we like it or not, in the direction of a global fusion, on a planet which is already too small for our ambitions and our dreams.'[1] Sound and image are both making the world a melting pot, and the ingredients cannot be separated again.

That raises the following question: in this irresistible and irreversible process, do the religions still have a role to play? Do they have anything to say? Or at a planetary level are they definitively superseded, outmoded, disqualified by their excesses, by the intolerances that they allow, the hatreds that they evoke, the murders that they inspire and the wars which are waged, here and there, with unparalleled ferocity, in their name and under their banner?

The writer Taslima Nasreen, who had to go into exile to escape a death threat from the 'Soldiers of God', makes one of her heroes remark: 'It is ironically said that all the religions have only one goal, peace. But it is in the name of religion that there has always been so much agitation, there have been so many conflicts; so much bloodshed, so many victims. It is indeed very regrettable that at the end of the twentieth century we are still witnesses to so many atrocities, all committed in the name of religion. Brandishing the banner of religion has always proved to be the means of reducing human beings to nothing as well as the spirit of humanity.'[2]

Yet the fact that the religions have been perverted in the service of the worst and that they continue to be so does not always prevent them from being purveyors of fundamental and inalienable values: they are the vehicles of the 'spirit of humanity'. The right to life, to a life of dignity, a fully human life, without discrimination, cannot seriously be put in question, although humankind began with a fratricide, a sad beginning which prefigured and presaged all our misfortunes, past and present. If there was fratricide, and always is, it is not legitimated by any religious ethic, properly understood.[3] In the Mishnah we read: '. . . if any man has caused a single soul to perish, Scripture imputes it to him as though he had caused a whole world to perish; and if any man saves alive a single soul, Scripture imputes it to him as though he had saved alive a whole world'.[4]

Echoing this text, and with an explicit reference to the 'children of Israel', we read in the Qur'an: 'Whoever kills a human being, except as a punishment for murder or other villainy in the land, shall be looked upon as though he had killed all mankind; and whoever saves a human life shall be regarded as though he had saved all mankind' (Surah 5.32). And there is no need here to dwell on the Golden Rule (Matt. 7.12; Luke 6.31), which exists in all the great religions. There is no need to pursue this theme further, even if it were possible to do so.

A world-wide process of growing awareness

The Declaration which was approved by the Parliament of the World's Religions in Chicago on 4 September 1993 has the merit of making representatives of all, or almost all, of the religions of the earth aware of their common heritage, a heritage which could form a quite solid platform for a global ethic. This Declaration also has the merits of clarity and conciseness. Like the Declaration on Human Rights, it could be a major event marking the end of our second millennium which, while perhaps 'agonizing', is still full of hope. If that were to happen, the Parliament of the World's Religions would need to be able to give itself permanent structures which would allow it to meet at regular intervals. It would need to become institutionalized. Why couldn't UNESCO provide the framework and the resources? The Parliament is an excellent forum within which all the religions could meet, exchange views, engage in dialogue and make proposals.

In fact, despite all the nostalgic resistance and all the anarchical diversions, from the beginning life has always been a process of evolution, certainly long and shaky, but sustained, towards an integration which is increasingly broad, increasingly global, consensual and intelligent. Today we have reached a point at which an ethic, however minimal, but global and planetary, has become an urgent necessity, vital for our survival in solidarity and for the pursuit of our mission on Planet Earth. An ethic is not a code of law. It is a code of obligations and duties. We have the Universal Declaration of Human Rights, but we do not yet have its necessary complement, the Universal Declaration of Human Obligations and Duties. The Parliament of Religions could prepare the way for it. From now on it has a charter, a framework to improve and fill out progressively. None of the articles of this charter poses any particular difficulties. But all the articles refer exclusively to interpersonal relations on a strictly horizontal plane. It is not necessary to have a religion to adhere to them fully. Believers and unbelievers meet here.

However, must the Parliament in this way ratify the dispossession of God from his creation, with the blessing *of all the religions*, in order to reach a consensus? Isn't this consensus detrimental to those who derive their ethic from God, an ethic which while being of this world is not only of this world? Nowhere is God mentioned in the Declaration. This absence is clearly not fortuitous. Buddhism has made a considerable contribution towards it. But wouldn't it be better to speak, rather, of a *contribution* from the religions to a minimal and *neutral* global ethic, and knowingly leave the door open for other adherents, non-believers in particular?

Were that to happen, it is clear that the Parliament would immediately lose its specific character, and cease to be a parliament of religions. We can see how difficult it is for the religions all to speak with the same voice. A formula needs to be found. Is that possible? If it is necessary, at whatever the cost, to silence God, to veil him, out of a sense of shame, I doubt it. This would be to change the perspective totally and opt for a pluralist parliament in which the religions found their place alongside other forms of thinking and living. Such a formula can certainly be envisaged, and is not necessarily bad in itself. But a parliament of religions which expresses itself in an atheistic way is nonsense.

Ethics for the religious and the non-religious

At a time when science is doing miracles, people everywhere are in fact in search of a universal ethic. For some this is a new ethic for a new age, that of genetic manipulation. For about a decade, cloning has made it possible to improve certain species of plants and animals. Very soon it will be extended to human beings. There is no doubt about that. Why not improve the human species, in principle as a priority? Why accept our nature as it has been made by human evolution? Why not change it, now that we have the means to do so, since we have almost deciphered the mystery of the genome? Why not immediately give ethics biological foundations?[5] Sociology has now been joined by sociobiology, and ethics have been joined by bioethics, not to mention information theory, which does not despair of creating artificial intelligence. In the near future people will no longer be able to think of ethics as it has been envisaged hitherto. There's a fine programme for all the religions!

In this context, by giving themselves a parliament, the religions have undoubtedly provided themselves with an indispensable arena for communal reflection in which they can first make peace between themselves and in themselves, and attain some harmony. That will be a difficult process in itself. But certainly they can no longer define the ethics of the future alone, for ethics is not only for believers. It is also for the others, who are increasingly influential by virtue of their thought and number. From now on ethics is a common affair. It involves all of us. No one can be isolated any longer; no one can escape contagion. The religions cannot be deaf to the voice of science, but they cannot abandon ethics exclusively to science or atheistic thought either.

As I have already noted, the fact remains that the religions cannot always speak with one and the same voice, since there are such profound differences, sometimes on essentials. Every global ethic must therefore take account of specifics. It is the same with human rights. In particular, faith, in the prophetic and monotheistic religions, is an individual commitment, a vertical and personal relationship to God. God also has rights. Anthropolatry is so pervasive that we tend to forget this. And human beings have more than rights. They also have duties, in a horizontal ethical relationship with one another, but also in a vertical relationship with God, a relationship of hope and free and trusting adherence.

For me as a Muslim, any ethic which does not integrate this vertical relationship, this transcendental dimension of my humanity, is untenable. It is limited to the rules of respectability and co-existence in solidarity and peace. That is good, but it is not enough. An ethic stripped of its transcendental dimension is flat; it does not strive upwards. It has no direction, no aim and no goal. It is simply well-ordered animality on earth. Human beings are more than that. It is the duty of the prophetic and monotheistic religions to say so, to bear witness to the fact. Then we must be ready to offer our hands to all.

Notes

1. M. Talbi, 'Une communauté de communautés. Le droit à la différence, et les voies de l'harmonie', *Islamochristiana*, Rome 1978, IV, 11.
2. T. Nasreen, *Lajja*, Paris 1994, 47f.

3. M. Talbi, 'Die Friedensbotschaft der Religionen aus der Sicht des Islam', in *Frieden – Gerechtigkeit – Entwicklung. Der Beitrag der Religionen zu einer Friedensordnung im Nahen Osten*, Sankt Augustin, October 1993, 30–42.

4. *The Mishnah*, ed. Herbert Danby, Oxford 1938, 388 (some versions have the words 'from Israel' following the occurrence of the words 'a single soul').

5. Cf. *Fondements Naturels de l'Éthique*, ed. Jean-Pierre Changeux, Paris 1994.

From the World of the Eastern Religions

Thoughts on the Parliament of the World's Religions

HAJIME NAKAMURA

The author, a professor in the University of Tokyo and now founder and director of the Eastern Institute, is one of the most distinguished historians of Buddhism

I feel it has a significant meaning for the history of mankind to organize the Parliament of the World's Religions 'Towards a Global Ethic'. I heartily welcome the idea of the 'harmony of religions and the modern world'. The dialogue among different religions is of great significance for promoting the mutual understanding of the peoples and contributing to a better future for the world. I sincerely wish the Parliament of Religions good success.

The one eternal religion in all religions

Today the conversation among various religions has become more expanded. Already in 1893, in the World's Parliament of Religions in Chicago, Vivekānanda, the representative from India, had an especially strong impact on the audience. He said:

> The seed is put in the ground, and earth and air and water are places around it . . . It becomes a plant, it develops after the law of its own growth . . .
> The case with religion is similar. The Christian is not to become a Hindu or a Buddhist, nor a Hindu or a Buddhist to

become a Christian. But each must assimilate the spirit of the others and yet preserve his individuality and grow according to his own law of growth.[1]

In retrospect, Vivekānanda reflected on the Chicago Congress and said that the Congress was a meeting that provided light to the future of humanity. According to him, the World's Parliament of Religions demonstrated to the world that holiness, purity and charity were not the exclusive possession of any church in the world, and that every system produced men and women of the most exalted character. In the face of such evidence, he further pointed out that if there is someone who dreams of the survival of his own religion and the perishing of the religions of others, he should be pitied. He should be told that, however hard he might try, there would be a time when people would write upon the banner of every religion such phrases as 'Help, not Fight', 'Assimilation, not Destruction', 'Harmony and Peace, not Dissension'.[2]

Apart from the various existing individual religions, Vivekānanda recognized the existence of one eternal religion that is something essential and common to all the religions. He said that the various religions of the world do not contradict or conflict with one another:

The religions of the world are not contradictory or antagonistic; they are but various phases of One Eternal Religion; that One Eternal Religion is applied to different planes of existence, is applied to the opinions of various minds and various races. There never was my religion or yours, my national religion or your national religion; there never existed many religions, there is only the one. One infinite religion existed all through eternity and will ever exist, and this religion is expressing itself in various countries in various ways. Therefore we must respect all religions and we must try to accept them all as far as we can. Religions manifest themselves not only according to race and geographical position, but according to individual powers. In one man, religion is manifesting itself as intense activity, as work. In another, it is manifesting itself as intense devotion, in yet another, as mysticism, in others as philosophy, and so forth. It is wrong when we say to other, 'Your methods are not right.'[3]

Scholars of Buddhism in East Asia (i.e., Chinese, Korean, Vietnamese and Japanese scholars) used to call what Vivekān-anda called 'One Eternal Religion' 'Shu', and what correspon-ded to each established religion 'Kyo'. There is a certain similarity between how the East Asian scholars grasped the truth and how Vivekānanda perceived the truth.

Rāmakrishna, the teacher of Vivekānanda, had already referred to the essence of religion:

Do not care for doctrines, do not care for dogmas, or sects, or churches, or temples; they count for little compared with the essence of existence in each man, which is spirituality; and the more this is developed in a man, the more powerful is he for good. Earn that first, acquire that, and criticize no one, for all doctrines and creeds have some good in them.[4]

After this World's Parliament of Religions, Vivekānanda organized the Ramakrishna Mission, and he devoted himself to the service of humanity. He reformed and developed Hinduism to be a world religion.

Buddhism gains new strength

This Chicago Congress also provided an opportunity for the renaissance or revitalization of Buddhism, demonstrating its true spirit. The Rev. Shaku Sōen and the Rev. Doki Hōryu participated in the conference as Japanese representatives. We know that this provided an opportunity for Buddhism to spread eastward towards the USA from Japan.

The Ven. Dharmapāla (1864–1933) of Sri Lanka represented Theravāda Buddhist tradition. When the ocean liner on which he was travelling arrived in Honolulu, a lady guest visited the Sri Lankan monk. She was Mrs Mary E. Foster (1844–1930), who was of Hawaiian royal descent. On meeting Dharmapāla, she received a kind of inspiration, being enchanted by the monk's holiness. She met the Ven. Dharmapāla only twice in her lifetime – on this occasion and again later in 1904. However, she donated her whole unimaginable fortune to the monk, which enabled the establishment of the Mahābodhi Society. The revival of Buddhism in India owes much to the activities of this organization.

Shinto becomes international

Shinto, the Japanese folk religion which existed even before the arrival of Buddhism through the Korean peninsula, has also responded to the ideological and religious currents of foreign countries, while maintaining its own characteristics.

Academic investigations by the late Professor Genchi Kato have proved that Shintoism also underwent a similar process of development to those of other religions. However, the fact that the essence of Shintoism is something beyond the discretion of trivial human existence had been experientially realized by Saigyō (1118–1190), a Buddhist poet. When the minstrel visited the Ise shrine to worship, he composed the following *tanka* (short poem).

> *Nanigoto no owashimasu kawa shiranedomo*
> *Katajikenasa ni Namida koboruru*
> (Who presides there, no one knows,
> overwhelming gratefulness fills my soul
> wetting my face with welling tears).

Broadly speaking, Buddhism and Shintoism are the two major religions in Japan. The essence of the two can be described as *magokoro* (a true heart). When this *magokoro* manifests itself, it is called *jihi* (*maitrī* and *karunā*, compassion). It is cited in one of the ancient Shinto verses:

> *Jihi no me ni nikushi to omou mono araji*
> *Toga aru mono wo nawo mo awareme*
> (For one who has compassionate eyes,
> no one worthy of hate exists.
> The sinful and the faulty
> should be viewed still more compassionately).

Or, in much simpler words, it can be described as *atatakai kokoro* (warm heart). If we detach ourselves from phenomena, and if we go into the realm of the 'essence', no discrimination exists.

World peace through the discovery of the nature of religion

If we view the external world from this supreme standpoint, war and strife will cease to exist. Then, the gate to the path leading to the realization of world peace will open. However, if we lose sight of this essential meaning of religion, then mankind will wage war in the name of religions, destroying and annihilating each other. If we observe this present-day world where we are making the most of the highly advanced technology produced by the advancement of scientific civilization, we find rampant cases of mass destruction and murdering under the name of religions. Further, the materialistic thought that goes against religion could bring about only massacre and rendering hardship to people. World peace can be achieved only when people can realize this real and essential meaning of religion.

Thus, owing to such considerations, I feel, the attempt of the Parliament of the World's Religions is most welcome to the Buddhists of the Far East and the South East. The discussions on the harmony of religions and the modern world has immeasurable importance for the future of mankind.

Notes

1. Swami Vivekānanda, *Chicago Addresses*, Calcutta 1991, 45–6.
2. Ibid., 46.
3. Id., *My Master*, Calcutta 1978, 57–8.
4. Ibid., 71.

As a Buddhist I Support . . .

A letter in a difficult situation

SULAK SIVARAKSA

The author is a champion of civil rights in Thailand and co-founder of the International Network of Engaged Buddhists in Bangkok

Dear Hans Küng,

Thank you for your letter of March 3. I am very much involved with the court case of *lèse majesté*, the verdict of which may come out by the end of this month, with a maximum punishment of fifteen years imprisonment, so I am not in a position to give a proper reaction or evaluation. However, I am all for the Declaration. Indeed I was involved with the draft with you at Tübingen prior to the World Parliament. I also supported it at the meeting of the World Conference of the Religions for Peace last year in Italy. Quite a number of people are not happy with the Declaration for various reasons, but for me, it is good that ethically we have a declaration agreed by a variety of personalities from different religious traditions and cultures. As a Buddhist, I wholeheartedly support the Declaration on a Global Ethic as promulgated by the Parliament of World's Religions in Chicago, in 1993.

With all my best wishes,

Yours sincerely,

Sulak Sivaraksa

The Charter of a Global Order

A message

L.M. SINGHVI

The author is High Commissioner of India for the United Kingdom in London

The Declaration toward a Global Ethic which emerged at the centennial meeting of the Parliament of World's Religions in 1993 in Chicago is a document of momentous significance. Many of the ideas incorporated into it were developed by Professor Küng in his book *Global Responsibility*, published in 1990 in German and in 1991 in English. In that book, he declared in words which sound prophetic, 'No survival without a world ethic. No world peace without dialogue between the religions.'

The Declaration of the World's Religions on a Global Ethic draws its basic ideas from different faith traditions and integrates them together to respond to the challenges of our embattled era of many crises. Those ideas are as old as the hills and as fresh and new as the day after tomorrow.

The Declaration encapsulates the distilled essence and wisdom of the dialogue in our own age and time. It has a profound contemporary thrust. It is suffused with the pain and the agony of the world in which we live, because 'Peace eludes us . . . our planet is being destroyed . . . neighbours live in fear . . . women and men are estranged from each other . . . children die!' The Declaration condemns the abuses of Earth's ecosystem; it condemns the poverty that stifles life's potential; it condemns the social disarray of the nations and the disregard for justice which pushes citizens to the margin; it laments the anarchy overtaking our communities. It beckons us to a global ethic and reassures us that the basis for a global ethic already exists. It affirms that a common set of core values, fundamental in the teachings of the religions, form the basis for the global ethic. It proclaims the interdependence of the peoples and the nations of the world. It asserts the principle of individual responsibility. It calls for a culture of solidarity and relatedness. It commits the world to a culture of non-violence, responsibility, justice and peace. It declares unequivocally: 'We shall not oppress, injure, torture or kill other human beings, forsaking violence as a means of settling differences.' It counsels humankind to strive for a just, social and economic order, to avoid prejudice and hatred, and to move beyond the dominance for power, prestige, money and consumption in order to make a just and peaceful world.

The abiding value of the Declaration lies, first, in identifying the fundamental crisis of the world, a crisis in global economy, global ecology and global politics. It lies, secondly, in the irrevocable and unequivical commitment to a culture of non-violence and respect for life, to a culture of solidarity and a just economic order, to a culture of equal rights and partnership between men and women. Finally, the Declaration has the potential of making a lasting contribution to humankind's tryst with destiny as a blueprint of a cross-cultural inter-faith bridge, as a covenant of human rights and obligations, and as a charter for a durable, meaningful, compassionate, just and peaceful global order.

Redefining Tolerance

DILEEP PADGAONKAR

The author was a member of the UNESCO Secretariat and Editor of The Times of India. *He is now President of Asia-Pacific Communication Associates*

The author, who was approached only in the last phase of the preparation of this book, could not write an extended commentary on the Declaration from an Indian perspective. However, he commented on his statement as follows: 'You will notice that I have not quoted a single specifically Indian text to back up my argument. That was a deliberate decision. The text manifestly represents the present consciousness of an Indian. This has been heightened by every possible influence: the influence of the language and culture of my region – Maharashtra – the different cultures of India and, not least, the world outside, especially the West. I believe not only in a pluralistic society, but also in a society in which every individual becomes richer by attaining pluralistic identities. I become anxious or feel alienated if some of these identities are threatened.'

With every passing day, the 'Declaration toward a Global Ethic' starkly reveals a trait which few had suspected it possessed when it was adopted in September 1993 at the end of the Council of the Parliament of the World's Religions: it has proved to be distressingly prescient. The Declaration drew a dark picture of the contemporary world, with its structural imbalances and asymmetries, its disparities and domineering urges. That picture has acquired darker hues in recent months.

The paradoxical situation of humankind

Stern paradoxes continue to confront humankind. Collectively, it has the knowledge, skills and means vastly to improve its material and spiritual conditions. Yet it is unable to eradicate even the most extreme forms of deprivation, alienation and fear.

It has the scientific and technological resources and the managerial acumen to produce goods and services on a staggering scale. Yet it lacks the will and imagination to distribute them in an equitable measure to all its constituents. It has failed to eliminate the thoroughly debilitating factors affecting large sections of the human species: hunger, ignorance and disease. Nor has it been able to contain ecological degradation.

Humankind's capacity to disseminate information and insight, often instantaneously, to virtually every point on our planet continues to expand hugely. This should, in theory, promote a heightened awareness of the world's diverse cultures. Unfortunately, despite the increasing capacity to exchange perceptions, the world is witness to the emergence of newer and more vicious forms of intolerance, in particular terrorism and religious bigotry.

The twin processes currently in vogue – globalization and decentralization – have given these paradoxes an edge of urgency. Globalization, particularly in economic matters, is meant to make goods and services affordable to the largest number of people possible, create more jobs and, thanks to the telecommunications revolution, give people access to each other. But it would be counter-productive if it paid no heed to the issues of social equity and cultural identity. Such globalization would further accentuate the divide between the well-endowed and less endowed peoples and nations of the world. It would perpetuate a West-centred parochialism driven by military might, economic clout and scientific and technological prowess.

Decentralization is designed to enable citizens actively to

participate in the making of decisions affecting their daily lives and to safeguard their cultures. But it can cause immense harm if it also becomes a synonym for parochialism. Decentralization must obviously not impede the free flow of ideas.

Unless the disparities and asymmetries are redressed and a balance is struck between the compelling processes of globalization and decentralization, more and more individuals will suffer the risks of exclusion and marginalization; societies will run the risk of implosion; and nations, which find it difficult to cope with the erosion of their sovereignty in the key areas of information flows and economic exchanges, will face the dangers of entropy. This was also the burden of the Declaration.

Strengthening common moral and spiritual values

In this context, tolerance, as the Declaration forcefully emphasized, is not only a moral imperative but the only efficacious strategy to negotiate through the paradoxes of the contemporary world. But this would require a redefinition of tolerance. Today, more than ever before, it cannot be construed as an acquiescence in, or an indifference to, the diversity of beliefs and ways of life and, even less, to the racial and gender prejudices and ideological and religious fanaticisms which so often give rise to terrorism.

Tolerance has to be defined in a more active and innovative manner. The experiences of multi-religious, multi-cultural and multi-racial societies, such as Indian society, spanning several centuries, demonstrate what the creative interplay between secular, moral and religious discourses can achieve: the ability to understand and empathize with the 'other' – or, more precisely, with the 'other's' ethical impulses – without renouncing one's own core beliefs and life-styles, and the willingness to balance the exercise of rights with responsibilities freely assumed.

Tolerance thus defined is an invitation to celebrate

humanity's manifold identities and, in the process, to strengthen the moral and spiritual values shared by them all: respect for life and the dignity of the individual and a relentless yearning for knowledge, freedom, justice and solidarity. Only then can it give the currencies of power – economic, military, scientific and technological – which regulate relations between individuals, communities and nations today the legitimacy and efficacy they lack at present.

Global Ethic – A Confucian Response

SHU-HSIEN LIU

The author is Professor of Philosophy at the Chinese University in Hong Kong

As I do not belong to any religious organization, I was not at the Parliament of the World's Religions in Chicago in 1993 which approved the text of a Declaration on a Global Ethic. But I accept with great pleasure the invitation to give my personal view of the Declaration, for like most of the representatives of the religions at this Parliament, I would not hesitate to put my signature to this document.

I would like to begin by observing that there is a Confucian contribution to the Parliament of the World's Religions, even if there was not a single Confucian group there. Thus for example the Confucian 'Golden Rule' was constantly cited as a cornerstone of the Declaration, and moreover a large number of the principles of Confucian ethics – as the fundamental doctrinal principles of the religious groups from the Far East – were accepted.

The great openness of Confucianism

This type of influence from Confucianism can perhaps also be illustrated by an investigation presented by a Korean scholar to an international conference in Singapore:[1] beginning with a government census of 1 October 1983, published in 1984, in which only two per cent of Koreans had described themselves as Confucians, Korean Gallup Inc. carried out a survey of a representative group of 400 people, supplemented by individual in-depth interviews to discover to what degree Koreans today still follow 'Korean rules of behaviour', like commemorating ancestors, respect for parents, regular rites at the tombs of ancestors, ceremonies commemorating the tribal ancestors of clans, and so on. The results are summarized in the following table

Religion	Acknowledged membership	'Confucianized' according to the results of the survey	%
Buddhists	77	77	100
Protestants	106	81	76.4
Catholics	20	18	90
Confucians	2	2	100
Others	6	5	83.3
No religion	189	183	96.8
Total	400	366	91.7

Even if serious methodological objections may perhaps be made to the way in which the survey was carried out, one thing is quite clear: although Confucianism in Korea is not very visible at present, almost all Koreans are Confucians. This is what the author then concludes:

The very fact that Confucianism was never an organized religion and never really laid claim to the absolute truth could now be an advantage for it, since it gives it the possibility of presenting its views in other parts of the world. In all probability Confucianism will never be an independent, unitary world religion. Instead of this it can seek to become the fundamental moral doctrine of human relationships by penetrating all religions and ideologies and being accepted by them, without coming into conflict with the foundations of a particular faith.

The spirit of such an interpretation of the Confucian message coincides completely with the aim followed by the

Parliament of the World's Religions. Since earliest times Confucianism has condemned the policy of attaining a position of dominance by military conquest or other forcible means. Men and women must strive for Confucian ideals quite voluntarily. The Neo-Confucian dictum *li-i-fen-shu* means that there is only one principle, but numerous manifestations of it. The favourite metaphor of Neo-Confucian philosophers was that the same moon shines over thousands of streams. Thus as well as Chinese Confucianism there is Korean Confucianism and Japanese Confucianism, and recently even a Boston Confucianism.[2] Moreover it is in no way necessary to remain within the limits of these forms of Confucianism. In short, at the Third International Conference on Contemporary Neo-Confucianist philosophy, held at the Chinese University of Hong Kong in December 1994, Tu Wei-Ming put the emphasis on the word 'Confucian' as an adjective. So one can be Confucian-Buddhist, Confucian-Christian and even Confucian-Muslim. This shows that the Confucian message has an openness which other religious traditions seldom allow. And Confucianism attaches the utmost importance to *ho*, to 'harmony', which is indispensable if we want to develop a global ethic for different peoples, nations, cultures and religions which they can live out peacefully in a world village without the 'Clash of Civilizations' which Samuel Huntington thinks probable.[3]

The problem of human rights in Asia

I am firmly convinced that the Confucian tradition contains great treasures which we must appropriate; however, that does not mean that there is nothing negative in this tradition. In fact in the course of its long history, after establishing itself as a binding state doctrine during the Han Dynasty, like other great world religions Confucianism gradually lost its original spirit. It was politicized and vulgarized, almost fossilized, and became the 'tradition of orthodoxy which devours men', to quote a condemnation of leading Chinese intellectuals from the turn of the century. It is an important mission of contemporary Neo-Confucian philosophers to regain the original spirit of Confucianism as embodied by Confucius and Mencius, by creative interpretation, and to discover its significance for the present. Thanks to their persistent efforts under extremely adverse conditions, contemporary Neo-Confucian scholars have become representatives of a view which can no longer be overlooked and which gained recognition even in China under Mao, as it has gained recognition overseas. Yet they would openly concede that despite the revival of the original spirit of Confucianism there are still limitations and deficiencies in this tradition which need to be taken seriously.

For example, the Chinese have not developed either modern natural science or democracy; concepts of freedom and human rights have not been sufficiently respected in China, in contrast to the West. The Chinese must make concessions to the West in order to broaden their horizons and enrich their culture. So I am not disturbed that the formulation of the Declaration on a Global Ethic is somewhat Western, as long as the spirit of the document does not undergo any such narrowing and the West makes concessions to the East or, better still, to the whole world. If we are to overcome our own limitations and deficiencies, we Asians must develop a concept of human rights in our own terms, even if the idea has its origin in the West, just as leading intellectuals in the West sound out their innermost depths and at the same time open their arms to all the other religious traditions of the world.

To be able to assess the strengths of other traditions is in fact a sign of one's own strength. We Confucians are lagging behind when it comes to the defence of human rights, but we have much to offer in connection with personal concern for a higher ethical awareness, which also makes an important contribution to bringing about social harmony and even world peace. We begin with inner personal development and then turn to human rights, whereas Hans Küng is urging us to go beyond the Declaration on Human Rights and approve the

Declaration on a Global Ethic. So we need not condemn our
own tradition – on the contrary, we are even called to revive
our tradition, for we are being urged not to neglect our ethical
conscience. In fact the highest ideal of the Chinese has always
been *nei-wi-ho-i*, 'the unity of inner and outer'. We were
certainly not in a position to realize this ideal. But is not such
an ideal precisely what we are all striving for when we declare
ourselves in favour of a global ethic which is common to all
world religions, in addition to the Declaration on Human
Rights?

Hope for a better world

I fully agree with Hans Küng that 'the Declaration on a Global
Ethic can offer only a minimal ethic. However, this does not
mean an ethical minimum. What it means is the minimum of
what the religions of the world already have in common
ethically, and which hopefully will be expanded and deepened
in the course of the process of communication.' We must try to
go still further, on both the theroetical and the practical levels.
The document signed in Chicago sets out only the principles of
a global ethic, and analytical philosophers will perhaps find it
wanting in theoretical subtleties. But this is a very promising
start for all of us, and both individuals and religious traditions
as a whole are called on to broaden and deepen their insights
and develop them into a coherent ethical system. On this
common basis we can then discuss among ourselves and learn
a great deal.

However, when it comes to realizing the ideals, I see no
rapid solution to the problem. The change in ethical awareness
certainly depends on arousing individuals, and this in turn
depends on training, not just the kind of education that we
receive in schools, but the formation of our own personalities
in a lifelong process of maturing. Families, churches and so on
can play important roles, both negative and positive. On the
one hand they must not be made instruments for spreading

feelings of hatred and bigotry; on the other hand they should help to broaden people's ethical consciousness. I have no doubt that the crisis which we face today threatens the existence of humankind and that it is very true that 'our earth cannot change for the better without a change in individual consciousness'. We must 'plead for an individual and collective change of consciousness, for a revival of our spiritual powers through reflection, meditation, prayer and positive thought, for a change of heart'. Together, can we move mountains? So at the end of my comments I must return to the example of Confucius, of whom it is said that he was one 'who works unswervingly towards a goal which he knows cannot be realized' (Analects XIV, 38). Only if we have this attitude, this hope, can we hope for a better world in the future.

Notes

1. Cf. Koh Byong-ik, 'Confucianism in Contemporary China', in *The Triadic Chord: Confucian Ethics, Industrial East Asia and Max Weber*, ed. Tu Wei-Ming, Singapore 1991, 184–202.
2. R. C. Neville, 'Confucianism as a World Philosophy. Presidential Address for the 8th International Conference on Chinese Philosophy (Beijing 1993)', *Journal of Chinese Philosophy* 21.1, 1994, 5–25.
3. S. P. Huntington, 'The Clash of Civilizations?', *Foreign Affairs* 72, no. 3, Summer 1993, 22–49. His problem is that for the most part he sees things from the perspective of a 'Realpolitik' and is not guided in his thoughts and actions by a vision from the sphere of the transcendent or a global ethic.

Towards a Culture of Peace and Development

AUNG SAN SUU KYI

The author is Leader of the Opposition in Burma and has been awarded the Nobel Peace Prize

The Nobel prize winner and Leader of the Opposition in Burma wrote this text for the UNESCO World Commission on Culture and Development, of which she has been an honorary member since the foundation of the organization in 1992, at the request of Javier Pérez de Cuéllar, the President of the Commission and former General Secretary of the United Nations. The text was then read out by Corazon Aquino, the former President of the Philippines, at a meeting of the Commission in Manila on 21 November 1994. Although since July 1989 Aung San Suu Kyi has been under house arrest in Manila with no contact with the outside world, since 1992 she has been allowed visits by members of the family. In June 1992 the World Commission on Culture and Development made a public appeal to the Burmese military government to release Aung San Suu Kyi, in which it pointed out that she was constantly being refused the basic freedoms guaranteed in the Universal Declaration on Human Rights, although Burma too had signed this declaration in 1948. Also in 1992 Aung San Suu Kyi, along with Julius K. Nyerere, was awarded the Simon Bolivar Prize. She has made this text available to us instead of a direct commentary on the Declaration on a Global Ethic, which is more than understandable, given her difficult situation. However, readers will themselves note how powerfully Aung San Suu Kyi, with her plea for human rights, democracy and cultural values, as a Buddhist represents the principles of a global ethic. While this book was going to press we received the welcome news that the house arrest on Aung San Suu Kyi has been lifted.

At its third meeting held at San José, Costa Rica, 22–26 February 1994, the World Commission on Culture and Development set itself three goals, the third of which was 'to promote a new cultural dynamic: the culture of peace and culture of development'. The Commission undertook to 'endeavour to recommend the concrete measures that could promote, on a national and international scale, a culture of peace' and went on to state that:

> a culture of peace, culture of democracy and culture of human rights are indivisible. Their effective implementation must result in a democratic management and ... the prevention of intercultural conflicts.[1]

Human development is more than economic growth

Peace as a goal is an ideal which will not be contested by any government or nation, not even the most belligerent. And the close interdependence of the culture of peace and the culture of development also finds ready acceptance. But it remains a matter of uncertainty how far governments are prepared to concede that democracy and human rights are indivisible from the culture of peace and therefore essential to sustained development. There is ample evidence that culture and development can actually be made to serve as pretexts for resisting calls for democracy and human rights. It is widely known that some governments argue that democracy is a Western concept alien to indigenous values; it has also been asserted that economic development often conflicts with political (i.e. democratic) rights and that the second should necessarily give way to the first. In the light of such arguments culture and development need to be carefully examined and defined that they may not be used, or rather, misused, to block the aspirations of peoples for democratic institutions and human rights.

The unsatisfactory record of development in many parts of the world and the ensuing need for a definition of development which means more than mere economic growth became a matter of vital concern to economists and international agencies more than a decade ago.[2] In *A New Concept of Development*, published in 1983, François Perroux stated that:

> Development has not taken place: it represents a dramatic growth of awareness, a promise, a matter of survival indeed; intellectually, however, it is still only dimly perceived.[3]

Later in the same book he asserted that:

> . . . personal development, the freedom of persons fulfilling their potential in the context of the values to which they subscribe and which they experience in their actions, is one of the mainsprings of all forms of development.[4]

His concept of development therefore gives a firm place to human and cultural values within any scheme for progress, economic or otherwise. The United Nations Development Programme too began to spell out the difference between growth and development in the 1980s.[5] With the beginning of the 1990s the primacy of the human aspect of development was acknowledged by the UNDP with the publication of its first Human Development Report. And the special focus of the 1993 Report was people's participation, seen as 'the central issue of our time'.[6]

While the concept of human development is beginning to assume a dominant position in the thinking of international economists and administrators, the Market Economy, not merely adorned with capital letters but seen in an almost mystic haze, is increasingly regarded by many governments as the quick and certain way to material prosperity. It is assumed that economic measures can resolve all the problems facing their countries. Economics is described as the '*deus ex machina*, the most important key to every lock of every door to the new Asia we wish to see'; and 'healthy economic development' is seen as

> . . . essential to successfully meeting the challenge of peace and security, the challenge of human rights and responsibilities, the challenge of democracy and the rule of law, the challenge of social justice and reform and the challenge of cultural renaissance and pluralism.[7]

The view that economic development is essential to peace, human rights, democracy and cultural pluralism, and the view that a culture of peace, democracy and human rights is essential to sustained human development, may seem on the surface to differ only in the matter of approach. But a closer investigation reveals that the difference in approach itself implies differences of a more fundamental order. When economics is regarded as 'the most important key to every lock of every door' it is only natural that the worth of man should come to be decided largely, even wholly, by his effectiveness as an economic tool.[8] This is at variance with the vision of a world where economic, political and social institutions work to serve man instead of the other way round; where culture and development coalesce to create an environment in which human potential can be realized to the full. The differing views ultimately reflect differences in how the valuation of the various components of the social and national entity are made; how such basic concepts as poverty, progress, culture, freedom, democracy and human rights are defined and, of crucial importance, who has the power to determine such values and definitions.

The value systems of those with access to power and of those far removed from such access cannot be the same. The viewpoint of the privileged is unlike that of the under-privileged. In the matter of power and privilege the difference between the haves and the have-nots is not merely quantita-tive, for it has far-reaching psychological and ideological implications. And many 'economic' concerns are seldom just that, since they are tied up with questions of power and privilege. The problem of poverty provides an example of the inadequacy of a purely economic approach to a human situation. Even those who take a down-to-earth view of basic human needs agree that:

> ... whatever doctors, nutritionists, and other scientists may say about the objective conditions of deprivation, how the poor themselves perceive their deprivation is also relevant.[9]

Are democracy and human rights in contradiction with national culture?

The alleviation of poverty thus entails setting in motion processes which can change the perceptions of all those concerned. Here power and privilege come into play:

> The poor are powerless and have no voice. Power is the possibility of expressing and imposing one's will in a given social relationship, in the face of any resistance. The poor are incapable of either imposing, coercing or, in many cases, having any influence at all.[10]

It is not enough merely to provide the poor with material assistance. They have to be sufficiently empowered to change their perception of themselves as helpless and ineffectual in an uncaring world.

The question of empowerment is central to both culture and development. It decides who has the means of imposing on a nation or society their view of what constitutes culture and development and who determines what practical measures can be taken in the name of culture and development. The more totalitarian a system, the more power will be concentrated in the hands of the ruling élite and the more culture and development will be used to serve narrow interests. Culture has been defined as 'the most recent, the most highly developed means of promoting the security and continuity of life'.[11] Culture thus defined is dynamic and broad, the emphasis is on its flexible, non-compelling qualities. But when it is bent to serve narrow interests it becomes static and rigid, its exclusive aspects come to the fore and it assumes coercive overtones. The 'national culture' can become a bizarre graft of carefully selected historical incidents and distorted social values intended to justify the policies and actions of those in power.[12] At the same time development is likely to be seen in the now outmoded sense of economic growth. Statistics, often unverifiable, are reeled off to prove the success of official measures.

Many authoritarian governments wish to appear in the forefront of modern progress but are reluctant to institute genuine change. Such governments tend to claim that they are taking a uniquely national or indigenous path towards a political system in keeping with the times. In the decades immediately after the Second World War socialism was the popular option. But increasingly since the 1980s democracy has gained ground. The focus on a national or indigenous way to socialism or democracy has

. . . the effect of stressing cultural continuity as both process and goal; this in turn obviates the necessity of defining either democracy or socialism in institutionally or procedurally specific terms; and finally, it elevates the existing political élite to the indispensable position of final arbiter and interpreter of what does or does not contribute to the preservation of cultural integrity.[13]

It is often in the name of cultural integrity as well as social stability and national security that democratic reforms based on human rights are resisted by authoritarian governments. It is insinuated that some of the worst ills of Western society are the result of democracy, which is seen as the progenitor of unbridled freedom and selfish individualism. It is claimed, usually without adequate evidence, that democratic values and human rights run counter to the national culture, and therefore to be beneficial they need to be modified – perhaps to the extent that they are barely recognizable. The people are said to be as yet unfit for democracy, therefore an indefinite length of time has to pass before democratic reforms can be instituted.

The first form of attack is often based on the premise, so universally accepted that it is seldom challenged or even noticed, that the United States of America is the supreme example of democratic culture. What tends to be overlooked is that although the USA is certainly the most important representative of democratic culture, it also represents many other cultures, often intricately enmeshed. Among these are the 'I-want-it-all' consumer culture, megacity culture, super-power culture, frontier culture, immigrant culture. There is also a strong media culture which constantly exposes the myriad problems of American society, from large issues such as street violence and drug abuse to the matrimonial difficulties of minor celebrities. Many of the worst ills of American society, increasingly to be found in varying degrees in other developed countries, can be traced not to the democratic legacy but to the demands of modern materialism. Gross individualism and cut-throat morality arise when political and intellectual freedoms are curbed on the one hand while on the other fierce economic competitiveness is encouraged by making material success the measure of prestige and progress. The result is a society where cultural and human values are set aside and money value reigns supreme. No political or social system is perfect. But could such a powerful and powerfully diverse nation as the United States have been prevented from disintegrating if it had not been sustained by democratic institutions guaranteed by a constitution based on the assumption that man's capacity for reason and justice makes free government possible and that his capacity for passion and injustice makes it necessary?[14]

Different peoples must agree on basic human values

It is precisely because of the cultural diversity of the world that it is necessary for different nations and peoples to agree on those basic human values which will act as a unifying factor. When democracy and human rights are said to run counter to non-Western culture, such culture is usually defined narrowly and presented as monolithic. In fact the values that democracy and human rights seek to promote can be found in many cultures. Human beings the world over need freedom and security that they may be able to realize their full potential. The longing for a form of governance that provides security without destroying freedom goes back a long way.[15] Support for the desirability of strong government and dictatorship can also be found in all cultures, both Eastern and Western: the desire to dominate and the tendency to adulate the powerful are also common human traits arising out of a desire for security. A nation may choose a system that leaves the protection of the freedom and security of the many dependent on the inclinations of the empowered few; or it may choose institutions and practices that will sufficiently empower individuals and organizations to protect their own freedom and security. The choice will decide how far a nation will progress along the road to peace and human development.[16]

Many of the countries in the Third World now striving for meaningful development are multiracial societies where there is one dominant racial group and a number – sometimes a large number – of smaller groups: foreign, religious or ethnic minorities. As poverty can no longer be defined satisfactorily in terms of basic economic needs, 'minority' can no longer be defined merely in terms of numbers. For example, it has been noted in a study of minorities in Burmese history that:

> In the process of nation-building . . . the notion of minority in Burma changed, as one group defines itself as a nation those outside the group become minorities.

There were, of course, minorities in traditional Burma – people close to the power elite who considered themselves superior and people estranged from the power elite who were considered inferior. These criteria for establishing majorities (who might in fact be a small portion of the population as, say, white people in South Africa today) were not based on race or even ethnic group, but on access to power. Minorities, thus, are those people with poor access to power.[17]

Once again, as in the case of poverty, it is ultimately a question of empowerment. The provision of basic material needs is not sufficient to make minority groups and indigenous peoples feel they are truly part of the greater national entity. For that they have to be confident that they too have an active role to play in shaping the destiny of the state that demands their allegiance. Poverty degrades a whole society and threatens its stability while ethnic conflict and minority discontent are two of the greatest threats to both internal and regional peace. And when the dispossessed 'minority' is in fact an overwhelming majority, as happens in countries where power is concentrated in the hands of the few, the threat to peace and stability is ever present even if unperceived.

The Commission for a New Asia notes that:

> . . . the most rapid economic transformation is most likely to succeed within the context of international peace and internal political stability, in the presence of social tranquil-lity, public order and an enlightened and strong govern-

ment; and in the absence of societal turbulence and disorder.[18]

This comment highlights the link between economic, political and social concerns. But there is a danger that it could be interpreted to imply that peace, stability and public order are desirable only as conditions for facilitating economic transformation rather than as ends in themselves. Such an interpretation would distort the very meaning of peace and security. It could also be used to justify strong, even if unenlightened, government and any authoritarian measures that such a government may take in the name of public order.[19]

If material betterment, which is but a means to human happiness, is sought in ways that wound the human spirit, it can in the long run only lead to greater human suffering. The vast possibilities that a market economy can open up to developing countries can be realized only if economic reforms are undertaken within a framework that recognizes human needs. The Human Development Report makes the point that markets should serve people instead of people serving markets. Further:

> . . . both state and market should be guided by the people. The two should work in tandem, and people should be sufficiently empowered to exert effective control over both.[20]

Human beings must be rated higher than power

Again we come back to empowerment. It decides how widespread will be the benefit of actions taken in the name of culture and development. And this in turn will decide the extent of the contribution such actions can make to genuine peace and stability. Democracy as a political system which aims at empowering the people is essential if sustained human development, which is 'development of the people for the people by the people', is to be achieved. Thus it has been rightly said that:

> National governments must find new ways of enabling their people to participate more in government and to allow them much greater influence on the decisions that affect their lives. Unless this is done, and done in time, the irresistible tide of people's rising aspirations will inevitably clash with inflexible systems, leading to anarchy and chaos. A rapid democratic transition and a strengthening of the institutions of civil society are the only appropriate responses.[21]

The argument that it took long years for the first democratic governments to develop in the West is not a valid excuse for African and Asian countries to drag their feet over democratic reform. The history of the world shows that peoples and societies do not have to pass through a fixed series of stages in the course of development. Moreover, latecomers should be able to capitalize on the experiences of the pioneers and avoid the mistakes and obstacles that impeded early progress. The idea of 'making haste slowly' is sometimes used to give backwardness the appearance of measured progress. But in a fast developing world too much emphasis on 'slowly' can be a recipe for disaster.

There will be as many kinds of democracies as there are nations which accept it as a form of government. No single type of 'Western democracy' exists; nor is democracy limited to a mere handful of forms such as the American, British, French or Swiss. Each democratic country will have its own individual characteristics. With the spread of democracy to Eastern Europe the variety in the democratic style of government will increase. Similarly there cannot be one form of Asian democracy; in each country the democratic system will develop a character that accords with its social, cultural and economic needs. But the basic requirement of a genuine democracy is that the people should be sufficiently empowered to be able to participate significantly in the governance of their country. The thirty articles of the Universal Declaration of Human Rights are aimed at such empowerment. Without these rights democratic institutions will be but empty shells incapable of reflecting the aspirations of the people and unable to withstand the encroachment of authoritarianism.

The democratic process provides for political and social change without violence. The democratic tradition of free discussion and debate allows for the settlement of differences without resort to armed conflict. The culture of democracy and human rights promotes diversity and dynamism without disintegration; it is indivisible from the culture of development and the culture of peace. It is only by giving firm support to movements that seek to empower the people through democratic means that the United Nations and its agencies will truly be able to promote the culture of peace and the culture of development.

The challenge to ally oneself with human rights

Let me in conclusion summarize my argument. The true development of human beings involves much more than mere economic growth. At its heart there must be a sense of empowerment and inner fulfilment. This alone will ensure that human and cultural values remain paramount in a world where political leadership is often synonymous with tyranny and the rule of a narrow elite. People's participation in social and political transformation is the central issue of our time. This can only be achieved through the establishment of societies which place human worth above power, and liberation above control. In this paradigm, development requires democracy, the genuine empowerment of the people. When this is achieved, culture and development will naturally coalesce to create an environment in which all are valued, and every kind of human potential can be realized. The alleviation of poverty involves processes which change the way in which the poor perceive themselves and their world. Mere material assistance is not enough; the poor must have the sense that they themselves can shape their own future. Most totalitarian regimes fear change, but the longer they put off genuine democratic reform the more likely it is that even their positive contributions will be vitiated: the success of national policies depends on the willing participation of the people. Democratic values and human rights, it is sometimes claimed, run counter to 'national' culture, and all too often the people at large are seen as 'unfit' for government. Nothing can be further from the truth. The challenge we now face is for the different nations and peoples of the world to agree on a basic set of human values, which will serve as a unifying force in the development of a genuine global community. True economic transformation can then take place in the context of international peace and internal political stability. A rapid democratic transition and strengthening of the institutions of civil society are the *sine qua non* for this development. Only then will we be able to look to a future where human beings are valued for what they are rather than for what they produce. If the UN and its agencies wish to assist this development they must support these movements which seek to empower the people, movements which are founded on democracy, and which will one day ensure a culture of peace and of development.

Notes

1. 'Draft Preliminary Outline of the World Report on Culture and Development', UNESCO, CCD-III/94/Doc. 2, Paris, 7 February 1994, 16.
2. It has been pointed out that the idea of growth, not as an end in itself but as a performance test of development, was put forward by economists as early as the 1950s: Paul Streeten et al., *First Things First: Meeting Basic Human Needs in the Developing Countries*, Oxford 1982.
3. François Perroux, *A New Concept of Development*, UNESCO, Paris 1983, 2.

4. Ibid., 180.

5. 'Growth normally means quantifiable measure of a society's overall level of production or incomes such as GNP or GDP per capita, while development involves qualitative aspects of a society's advancement such as under- and un-employment, income distribution pattern, housing situation, nutritional level, sanitary condition, etc.': *UNDP Selected Sectoral Reviews: Burma December 1988*, 333.

6. *Human Development Report 1993*, UNDP, Oxford 1993, 1.

7. *Towards a New Asia*. A Report of the Commission for a New Asia, 1994, 39.

8. 'The logic of an economy governed by solvency and by profit, subject to the increasing value attached to capital and to the power of those who command it, is to reject as 'non-economic' everything which cannot be immediately translated into quantities and prices in market terms': Paul-Marc Henry (ed.), *Poverty, Progress and Development*, London 1991, 36.

9. Streeten et al., *First Things First (n. 2)*, 19.

10. Henry (ed.), *Poverty, Progress and Development* (n. 8), 34.

11. *The New Encyclopaedia Britannica*, Chicago 1993, Vol. 16, 874.

12. Edward Said comments that governments in general use culture as a means of promoting nationalism: 'To launder the cultural past and repaint it in garish nationalist colours that irradiate the whole society is now so much a fact of contemporary life as to be considered natural.' See id., 'Nationalism, Human Rights, and Interpretation', in Barbara Johnson (ed.), *Freedom and Independence: The Oxford Amnesty Lectures 1992*, New York 1993, 191.

13. Harry M. Scoble and Laurie S. Wiseberg (eds.), *Access to Justice: Human Rights Struggles in South East Asia*, London 1985, 57.

14. See Clinton Rossiter's introduction to Hamilton, Madison and Jay, *The Federalist Papers*, Chicago 1961. I owe thanks to Lady Patricia Gore-Booth for the original quotation on which Rossiter presumably based his words: 'Man's capacity for justice makes democracy possible; but man's inclination to injustice makes democracy necessary', from Reinhold Niebuhr's foreword to his *Children of Light and Children of Darkness: A Vindication of*

Democracy and a Critique of its Traditional Defence, London 1945.

15. 'The best government is that which governs least' are the words of a Westerner, John L. O'Sullivan, but more than a thousand years before O'Sullivan was born it was already written in the Lao Tzu, a Chinese classic, that 'the best of all rulers is but a shadowy presence to his subjects'. The notion that 'in a nation the people are most important, the State is next and the rulers the least important' is to be found not in the works of a modern Western political theorist but in that of Mencius.

16. Ehran Naraghi has shown in his memoirs *From Palace to Prison: Inside the Iranian Revolution*, London 1994, that a critical attitude towards the monarch, decentralization of power and division of responsibilities were part of oriental tradition. His fascinating conversations with Shah Mohammed Reza Pahlavi throw into relief the dangers of cultural and development policies divorced from the aspirations of the people.

17. Ronald D. Renard, 'Minorities in Burmese History', in K. M. de Silva et al. (eds.), *Ethnic Conflict in Buddhist Societies: Sri Lanka, Thailand and Burma*, London 1988, 79.

18. *Towards a New Asia* (n. 7), 40.

19. 'Practically any human behaviour can be, and historically has been, rationalized as threatening to damage the security of the nation', Scobie and Wiseberg (eds.), *Access to Justice* (n. 13), 58.

20. *Human Development Report 1993* (n. 6), 53.

21. Ibid., 5. Scobie and Wiseberg (eds.), *Access to Justice* (n. 13), 5, point out the difference between fundamental reform that 'involves a redistribution of power, a broadening of participation and influence in the making of authoritative decisions' and contingent reform that 'involves a sharing of the benefits of power holding, or the uses of power, in order to avoid the sharing of power itself'.

On the Establishment of a Global Ethic Foundation

COUNT K. K. VON DER GROBEN

After I came across Hans Küng's book *Global Responsibility*, I kept thinking how the notion of a global ethic, which fascinates me, could be disseminated.

I have had the good fortune to have lived my 'first life' in the patriarchal world of the East. Here there were still fixed ethical values and 'rules of the game' in which people had been brought up for generations. This ended with the Russian invasion, when I and my wife rode westwards through our forest.

In the 'second life' which then began I have had both good fortune and success, and can look back with gratitude on a full life. Now it is my wish to do something for people today who no longer have a firm basis of fixed values and are engaged in a search for them. So I want to help to further the ideas of a global ethic.

To this end, together with Professor Küng I have created the Global Ethic Foundation. It is to be devoted to inter-cultural and inter-religious research, education and encounter.

Its aim is to show that there are more satisfying values than material pleasure, and that to commit oneself to a lofty goal brings great joy.

We must get away from the celebration of 'self-fulfilment' and the idea of prosperity and make it clear to people that if we are to live together in peace and freedom we need high ethical norms.

Perhaps yet more people will associate themselves with our initiative. There is plenty of work and plenty to do.

The aims of the Foundation are:

I. To carry out and encourage **inter-cultural and inter-religious research**:

This aim will be achieved in particular through the production and promotion of academic publications (books and articles) in the interest of inter-cultural, inter-religious and inter-confessional understanding.

II. The stimulation and implementation of **inter-cultural and inter-religious education**:

This aim will be achieved in particular through:

– Publicity about a global ethic with the help of the media (newspaper articles, interviews, radio and television broadcasts);
– Lectures to disseminate the idea of a global ethic in churches, schools, colleges, associations, parties and interested groups of every kind, national and international;
– Further education of those interested, through conferences, lectures, seminars or workshops aimed at deepening the themes of a global ethic.

III. The enabling and support of **inter-cultural and inter-religious encounter**:

This aim will be achieved in particular by:

– The stimulation and encouragement of initiatives in society, politics and culture aimed at understanding between peoples (e.g. measures to build up trust between the religions);
– Promotion of encounters between people of different cultures and religion (individual contacts, colloquia, study trips and congresses);
– The development of the existing network of inter-cultural and inter-religious relations to further a change of consciousness in the direction of a global ethic;
– The use of the possibilities of modern communication

technologies (e.g. Internet) in the service of the aims of the Foundation.

The Foundation will be based in Tübingen.

Secretariat: Global Ethic Foundation,
Waldhäuser Strasse 23,
72076 Tübingen,
Germany.